Wild Flowering of Girls
Gail Burkett, Ph.D.

Girls and wildflowers, unique and astonishing,
As they grow, intimate relationships open.
Their beauty depends on environment and weather conditions.
Sometimes critters eat them, bugs carve holes and leave them.
Bending in the rain, flowers and girls learn about resistance,
Forceful winds challenge their resilience.

In the early Spring of their life
Little yellow Pudica leaves and petals shining
Push perfected through crusty snow webs,
Stretching for potential, they learn boundaries.
Pirouette to stun the heart and dazzle the mind,
Girls' bodies change before the spin ends.

Each bud cries the tears of hope to bloom,
Circles of light, water, and love create blossoms to admire.
Delicate, colorful, sweet smelling, young girls' smiles
Melt every soul, one by one, each heart.
Rose is not Gaillardia is not Violet,
Who cares for them, wildflowers and girls?

Woman's spirit remembers passion,
Spurts of growth, blooms, seeds, dormancy,
Seasons turn into surrender and transformation.
Spring blooms eternal, for in the heart of every woman
Lives the hopeful bud of a girl with an answer:
Girls need women to be wise, thorough, trust-mates.

How much of our wild flowering do we remember?

Gifts from the Elders

Gifts from the Elders

Girls' Path to Womanhood

Gail Burkett, Ph.D.

iUniverse, Inc.

New York Lincoln Shanghai

Gifts from the Elders
Girls' Path to Womanhood

iUniverse, Inc.

For information address:
iUniverse, Inc.
2021 Pine Lake Road, Suite 100
Lincoln, NE 68512
www.iuniverse.com

ISBN: 0-595-32454-1

Printed in the United States of America

To Kenny, my playmate, with love!

For Dee and Lauren, may you lead the way to a New Story for
Womanhood.

Contents

ACKNOWLEDGEMENTS

For **all** my loved ones, especially my sisters, I treasure you and I am thrilled that you are secure and balanced in your womanhood. I ask now that you own your role in my journey and know how much you have helped me—immensely! You have wiped my tears and hugged me until my energy shifted, you have brainstormed with me until my way clearly appeared, you have laughed with me and entertained me, most of all, you have played with me. Through our play together, we will always be able to define ourselves and we will always be connected by our heart-strings. Thank you for helping me to grow into the woman I am and thank you for placing me on my path as elder-becoming. Because of our combined efforts, I am clear that my purpose is a great give-away—helping mothers and daughters form circles to nurture, support, and prepare young girls for womanhood.

Sisters by choice, Diana Eldridge, Kathleen Bjorkman-Wilson, Lorene Wapotich, Gaynol Wapotich, Alexandra Delis-Abrams, Erin Roper, Nancy Smith, Jade Sandoval, and Jo Davison, you are my bright stars. For my daughter, Dee Campbell thank you for being and showing me how to be all that we can be. Krista, your magical laughter has made this effort so sweet, thank you for sharing Una's pirouettes with me. Thank you Lauren, you led the way and were such a shining inspiration.

Thanks especially to my mentors, may you understand how much your counsel has guided me—Susan Morgan, Sharon Sweet, Joe Meeker, Rick Medrick, Dolores LaChapelle, and too many authors to name, especially Carol Gilligan, Clarissa Pinkola Estés, Susan Griffith, and Jean Shinoda Bolen. Finally, thank you Sue Katz, for applying your wordsmith talents. With the help of all of my mentors and friends, I am changing and growing every day.

You gain strength, courage, and confidence by every experience
in which you really stop to look fear in the face.
You must do the thing which you think you cannot do.

—Eleanor Roosevelt

Prologue

Did the women in your life prepare you for the roles and responsibilities of womanhood? For haunting questions, we must be brave enough and quiet enough to listen for answers. For me, the Divine Feminine responded with a challenge. Girls we know, daughters, nieces, and friends, need to be given or taught all the special components of womanhood. So many of the key components that create a woman's life were not given to me or even modeled for me when I was eight or ten or twelve. Girls need womanhood training so that each of them need not reinvent the archetypal parts. This give-away is the challenge I have accepted as my purpose. Do you remember when the doorway opened and invited you to pass over the threshold into your full womanhood bloom?

I had been so lost when I left the family nest. For me, the decades flew past. Finally, now I understand the complexities and all the efforts that goes into our definition of womanhood. Women must work so hard to individuate and separate from our mothers and then reunite because good relationships do blend interdependence with independence. What a challenge I have accepted, what a responsibility to redefine girlhood as a training opportunity for womanhood! Imagine the difference in girls' lives in just one generation if women closest to them offered the gift of awareness and skills to unlock the essence of their womanhood. The metamorphosis of womanhood, empowered teens, the splendor of our gender, this is a dream worthy of our consideration.

Women must own our true magnificence. We need to have the courage to pass wisdom down to the youngest generation. Girls from eight

1

to eighteen desperately need the offering of women's experience—our *generativity*—the passing of wisdom between generations as Angeles Arrien describes in *The Second Half of Life*. Women need to gather wisdom in a bundle and offer it to girls because that will heal the spiritual hole in every woman's adolescence. Our collective purpose is to answer the haunting question, what is the legacy of womanhood?

I spent two and a half years alone at 8000 feet on a Colorado mountainside. Through the miracle of technology and distance learning degrees, I completed a Masters degree in Adolescent Development. In the middle of my life, I became interested and introspective—I wanted to know why I had felt so lost since my early adolescence. I read all of Howard Gardner's work and walked in the woods so his theory of multiple intelligences could sink into my bones. He claims everyone is like me. People only acquire true knowledge when we apply multiple methods to the learning process. Unaided, reading or hearing are usually insufficient to attach to our neurological scaffold or brain patterns. People normally *blend* eight methods of learning. Individually, learning styles are all unique. After Gardner, I read Susan Harter's adolescent studies and sang with delight because I finally understood self-esteem and developmental cessation. Through all of my academic studies, Carol Gilligan's relational listening method exposed the patriarchal wall that quiets the voices of adolescent girls worldwide. Her writings unlocked the mysteries of adolescent girls, the one I had become so detached from in my own story and those girls I reach out to now. Many more mentors led me down the path to doctoral studies. In the world today, women's choices are unlimited. My choices blended Women's Studies with Natural History for a double emphasis Ph.D. My continuing research on adolescent Rites of Passage will always be the wind in my sails.

In order to evolve as spiritual beings, our culture must alter the free-for-all known as adolescence. A powerful motivator can be found in initiations. If adults don't provide them, young people will continue to initiate each other through dares. A carefully planned journey to adulthood is preferable to the hazards of sex, drugs and alcohol abuse.

Confident young girls, who feel acceptance as a woman by their family and friends, will be at almost zero risk with their peers. Through ceremony, girls will understand that important sense of belonging in their souls. They won't need to prove their womanhood to boys through pregnancy, drinking alcohol or accepting drug dares.

Girls' path to womanhood is explored in this book. By looking deeply into the foundation of womanhood and celebrating initiation rituals, women's wisdom will be reclaimed. Kin to the bedrock of this earth and to cultural and planetary well-being, womanhood must be earned and bestowed upon young women for them to stand in their own power. The heart of each young girl needs to feel the unwavering support of her family and friends. Girls are mostly unaware of their creative powers to gather women for celebration and sharing of wisdom. Just as young girls have created a demand to develop their beauty, for wholeness, girls also need women's wisdom to help them develop courage and competence. Looking into their souls, we need to respond to those unspoken demands by sharing our experience. Together, women and girls can gather the best ceremonies from our ancestors, our intuitive memories, and from our creative juices to build a bridge to the future to strengthen the foundation of womanhood.

Girl babies are all through my family tree, so this book is offered specifically to young girls who straddle the Millennium, who are related by blood or choice, all of whom are adopted and loved, totally. Together, let's look into the eyes of Millennial Girls and ask them what they need. Of course we must then be prepared to listen. The process of becoming women is so very complex, and as we grow together, our womanhood needs will be like an ever-blooming rose, layered, enduring, and so sweet. In quiet reflection, there is much to understand about our stories—our personal her-stories. We can invoke the grandmothers, our own ancestors lined up all the way back to the Ancient Ones. The ancestral grandmothers will help us see through the centuries, to peer into the pain and confusion of our childhood and adolescence, to understand the level of forgiveness we need. Our imaginations will blend with simpler times to create womanhood trainings and Rites of Passages as methods for healing and prevention.

All women who now have an extraordinary daughter or granddaughter, niece or grandniece, or a girl from a dozen other relational descriptions, this book is for you. Women have important gifts these girls need. We only need to look to our roots. What about womanhood have we worked hard to create or invent that we might have been taught?

As I healed my adolescent wounds with a mixture of academic studies and soulful, new understanding, a passion began to rise. In full and glorious bloom now, that passion is about giving girls a solid foundation for their womanhood, a foundation filled with enduring *wisdom, skills, and relationships.* Those three things combine for a powerful support system for eighteen year old women. Just like society provides public schooling on a consistent basis, girls need women to teach them so much more about womanhood. As a gift to the girls from eight to eighteen, their paths to adulthood need more women, more often. Girls need thousands of connection threads that come to us through our genes. Those sacred inborn characteristics identified as feminine—our bodily curves, our ability to birth new life from our ancient gene pool, how to use our intuitions and our gentle natures, be nurturing and receptive toward all our relations—these gifts and others weave together to make us female. Those are the connections the girls need, women's relationship connections.

Through these chapters we will deepen our connection to ourselves, to other kindred spirits, back to the grandmothers and forward to the unborn. When women recognize our innate commitment to the babies of the future we cannot name, the Eighth Generation, then all of womanhood will be recreated and transformed through the New Story we offer now for the future. We have memories to share and more to make, as our ancestors did. We will relearn to make time to share stories and parables. As we remember through our own lens what girls need, we will explore how to make connections so we truly hear their words, their pain, their celebrations. We will form thriving relationships through nature mentoring and the spirit of play. We will offer the natural passage ceremonies, Puberty Rites and Rites of Passage, as the gifts which create maturity. We will plan events, celebrations, and challenges to share wisdom about womanhood. So much goes into the individual creation of each woman. This is only the beginning. Cultural evolution is required to establish a New Story for womanhood. Looking back, not all of the recent cultural evolvement has been positive for girls or the women who love them. I recommend we take an active role to bundle women's evolution with tools that are thoughtful and methods that are cooperative.

An important part of this conscious evolution, the New Story for womanhood we co-create, will be women's circles for girls. Women will offer challenges unique to each specific girl. Individually, each girl will be sent outdoors to develop her knowledge of the Earth, and to amass dirt time, to create opportunities for sitting in and exploring her natural world. Through the quiet time in Nature, she will learn about herself. Each girl also needs to accept challenges designed just for her to explore and expand her creative passions and service to her community. Each chapter is offered to women-becoming as a gift from the elders. I wish that Millennial Girls be given circles and ceremonies to gently cultivate their maturity. From the heart of women's circles, wisdom of the Divine Feminine will provide the unique guidance of choice for this offering. Women, this is for you too. We are inventing something new together, this is the New Story of girls' path to womanhood.

1

Dancing With the Ancestors

Our bodies are only the cocoon and our souls are the butterfly.
When the time is right to die the cocoon releases the butterfly.

—Elisabeth Kubler-Ross

† † †

To create an enduring bond, I begin with the Ancestral Grandmothers. If women want to design a bright and hopeful vision for our future, we must connect to the past for our humanity—both for stories and for our ancestors' wisdom. The grandmothers symbolize a natural womanhood that has been lost, so to call forth and make a connection to the Ancient Ones, we must use our imaginations. We seek a model for how to come together in relationships, how to grow native to our place and how to learn the lessons we need to remain in balance. Natural womanhood demonstrates how to live harmoniously and with deep respect in the circle of life. For instance, how do we connect to the Divine Feminine for the guidance we need? How do we feel and teach reverence for Mother Earth? These answers are found in ancestral ecology. For answers to many questions, we only need to reclaim the connection to our own intuitive memories and our wisdom within.

In truth, the model rises as much from imagination as from the Ancestors. Before recorded history, the grandmothers were women who talked and laughed as we do. They cooked and sewed as we do. They provided shelter and tended nature's garden as we do. Their lives were easy by their standards and difficult by ours. I prefer to imagine, through a lens of ease, that there were many women's hands working together to provide food, clothing, shelter, care and ceremony for the village. To keep themselves whole, they spent solitary time in Nature. They sat in the Moon Lodge with the other women who were menstruating. There they nurtured themselves as they nurtured their tribe. Women lived in cooperation with the men of the village, each gender able to cross over to the other. Men helped with building shelters and gathering plants, and, when needed, women helped with the hunting. Both performed the ceremonies and kept the seasonal calendars. They are now known as the hunter-gatherers. When we lay down old assumptions, we see that men and women were both hunters and gatherers.

For reference, I stand on the shoulders of scholars Paul Shepard and Marija Gimbutas. I feel deeply indebted to the miracle of their cumulative efforts. From completely different perspectives, separately and respectively, they provided a synthesis for the hunter-gatherers and the Goddess cultures to feed our imaginations. Actually, they each stepped over the barrier of 10,000 years into prerecorded times. Beyond the gap of recorded history, way back in time, before too much civilization and certainly before agriculture, there is where I think we can trace our genetic expectations and connect to our intuitive memories.

Through their many books, Marija Gimbutas and Paul Shepard, added clarity to my vision of the Ancient Ones. They both left massive bodies of research for us to contemplate. Marija Gimbutas was raised in a tiny holding of village people and observed the old ways before World War II. She used her native sensibilities to peer back in time to the Goddess Cultures of 8,000 and 10,000 B.C.E. Among the artifacts unearthed in her archeological expeditions, she discovered many thousands of sculptures of woman with peaceful and gentle poses who were adorned, nude, and/or pregnant. Marija was fascinated that she found almost no sculptures of men and no sign of weapons in her excavations. Women were clearly in a position of prestige before the rise of patriarchy. Now, years after her death, through her books, we gain a clear view of the matrilineal culture that reigned throughout the Mediterranean region. Many of our own genetic lines can be imagined back to those matriarchs.

Paul Shepard painted a lucid picture of the Ancient Ones because he hoped their ways could be reclaimed to heal the Earth and slow the rate of species extinction. My passion has become entwined with Shepard's. First, I agree that we need to raise the next generations of children to experience and enjoy their fullest potential and their true maturity. Second, we must seek ways to restore the Earth to a self-sustaining balance. Unlike the Ancient Ones who always revered their ancestral lineage, we no longer hold them in our worldview. In *Coming Home to the Pleistocene* Shepard wrote, "Lacking a sense of the spiritual presence of plants and animals and of non-living matter, we do not feel our ancestors watching or their lives pressing on our own as did prehistoric peoples."

Our ancestral lineages can be traced to the lushest garden spots around the planet. There is no question that the Ice Age pushed the limits of survival, but until the Ice receded, populations were small and either nomadic or semi-nomadic. The fine points of our Ancestors' lives are veiled in obscurity, including where and how they lived. We are comforted to know they lived small-village tribal lives in Africa, Asia, Australia, Europe and North America. In childhood and youth, between the ages six and sixteen, they were offered skills training. Each person needed to be self-sufficient, to know all there was to know about the natural world, and to achieve a mastery that made their tribe stronger. Girls learned to hunt the small animals with dependable success and boys gathered precisely the plants their mothers needed from distant fields. They became whatever their heart's desired—basket weavers or pottery makers, bow craftsmen or master trackers, healers or shaman.

We've moved centuries beyond the hunter-gatherers. Girls of today have layers of complexity to navigate. They need self-sufficiency in order to cultivate self-esteem; they need to know the natural world for wholeness and balance; and they need a much stronger web of womanhood support through all their developmental years, from eight to twenty eight. The Ancient Ones brought eight year-old girls into their women's circles. As a strong and sure network of support was woven above, beneath and around them, girls learned survival skills. They were shown how to carefully gather and store food and medicines, and they discovered their spiritual power during their menses.

Together, let's look into the eyes of each of our young girls and see if we can answer this question, "What does she need? What does she need that I did not receive?" A question with that kind of mystery is really a question for our souls. The spirit in this book is dedicated to all of our girls—those who are related by blood or choice, as well as those adopted by our hearts and loved deeply. Imagine the most beautiful web, shimmering in the sunlight, linking together women and girls across the country. This New Story is ours to coax out of the ashes of time.

♀ ♀ ♀

Our Elders knew something we often want to deny. Everything changes when girls turn eight years old. The year that represents the late childhood stage of their development, eight is also the year that hormones are first produced by the body. Women know what hormones mean. From the Moon cycle to moodiness, our ovarian hormone, estrogen, is central to the chemistry that makes us feminine instead of masculine. Your nine or ten year old girl may be like I was, very much a tomboy. The term androgynous means balanced, but I went the other direction. I was not clearly defined as a girl, no pink stuff for me. I could do anything the boys could do, only better. That was true through the sixth grade, but after that I lost my edge. Not only did I lose my edge, I became self-conscious, embarrassed about my changes and poorly supported. My mother rests in peace because we talked this through before she passed, but I needed much more support than I received. I needed many more conversations than we had.

Before I did any of the research for my thesis on mother/daughter relationships, I interviewed over a hundred women about their childhood and adolescent years. Those women agreed that their needs were not met. They spoke of the wisdom, "You can't give what you didn't receive." Our mothers didn't receive womanhood training, either. Each of those women, one by one, reinvented womanhood for herself. From that void after their war-time work, our mothers created the first "too busy" generations persisting today. With conscious awareness, we will not raise another generation filled with too much busyness. The busy mantra marks death for creativity or at least a deep wounding. This awareness weaves wisdom threads around careful listening to girls' needs to create a safe vessel for womanhood training.

The saying "there is no end to women's work" also holds true for men, who are our vital partners in this dance we call life. (I would mention here as an aside that men need to provide this kind of relationship training for themselves and for boy children.) Together, women and men need to examine ways to raise the next generations of children in closer relationship with the Earth. The crucial work of our lives is the gift of maturity, centered around the relationships we hold most dear—our relationships with ourselves, with other people, and with the life on this planet. We hope that the experiences of love and trust, of play and joy, of reverence and wholeness, will reach around the globe and into the hearts of every human being. For that to happen as we envision, we must take action. Our work will never be complete, but what a blessing to give-away our wisdom.

The Ancient Ones are somehow related to us, although we've forgotten. So much time has passed that our memories cannot recall the oldest of our direct ancestors. Their stories don't even live in most of us, and we hardly ever think of them. Yet, if we could trace our lineage way back, our gift would be a deeper sense of ourselves. Good imaginations will have to do that tracing because we want to go back far enough to discover where our own natural roots were severed. There's a healing waiting for us in those roots where we were once in full accord, in total harmony with the earth, in balance from mind to body to spirit, and free to be our whole selves within our tribe. Our old Ancestors provided our genetic pool, which gives us a powerful way to know them. We only need to sit quietly and look inside. Can you locate the time when your bloodline relations lived off the land in unity with the Earth and all her wild living things?

When I tried to respond to this question myself, I began with the Ancient Ones who lived on the Earth before written records or agriculture. Then, looking to relations in my own family tree, I found Great-grandmother Sophia Bledsoe smiling down on me. Full Cherokee from Carolina, she walked the Trail of Tears holding hands with my Grand-dad Harry Burkett. Sophia has guided and invigorated this work. She's the genetic intuition that whispers to me. I have dreamed with Sophia, her spirit has quickened and deepened my passion. In my dreams she has told me the Divine Feminine calls to all women at this time.

Let's do some spying on village life. We can barely sense the time when all women were "mothers" in the village. Children knew their birth mothers and they were equally confident that every other woman would give them protection and sustenance. With sufficient silence, perhaps you can bring to mind such a time in your own lineage. You may imagine your lineage before written history, when harmony reigned all around the planet, when women knew their place, when men knew their place and cooperation eased survival. Maybe your native lineage is recent, when your people lived in rapport with all living things. Still, all that remains to you and me are pieces, like pottery shards—small bits of stories, memories, a knowing.

Sustainable skills for living from the Earth were developmental progressions that followed walking and running. Children first learned to be nature watchers and fire makers. Then they became fire tenders, gatherers, cooks, house builders, tool-makers and finally hunters. Little children were androgynous, they were gender balanced and raised with no differentiation until age eight.

This is where we might delve deeply into village life for pearls of wisdom. We want to know how children might be raised and what gifts might be remembered forward into our 21st Century. Gregory Cajete has helped us with this visioning. In *Look to the Mountain: An Ecology of Indigenous Education,* his research and writings have reclaimed native teachings for his people. By the time children reach the pivotal age of late childhood, they already know their world in detail. All of the plants and animals are their intimates. They are schooled in plant lore by the aunties and grandmothers, and in animal lore by the uncles and grandfathers. Not only do they know the names of every one of their nature relations, they know seasonal peculiarities, the uses of the plants, as well as the methods for gathering and storing food, so they can reliably respond to the needs of the village. If the tribal healer needs Pipsessewa, any one of the children is able to gather the amount needed.

Until girls and boys are invited to broaden their view, they remain focused on childhood play, except for ceremonial times, when they absorb the rare view of the village people together as a whole unit. Every tribal member participated in all the celebrations of birth, naming, initiation rituals, marriage, death and the seasonal festivals. From the periphery, the children watched. They watched and waited, often whispering to each other. There were some privileges that came with being a child, such as freedom to roam, to play, to run far with the wind. There were some privileges that came with growing older, such as participating in the celebrations and sacred ceremonies of the village, and sitting in the elders' council circle. At the pivotal moment in their development when girls received an invitation to sit with women, they knew their time as children had come to an end.

When a child reached his or her eighth season counted from birth, the Grandmothers and Grandfathers held a council over her or his future. One of the elders stepped forward to offer to be that child's personal guide. For the girl children, the ones we are most curious about in this project, that mentor was always an older woman, maybe a true Grandmother, but always other than Mother. For the boy children, their mentor was always a man, an uncle or Grandfather. While the children were impressionable, the Elders were intimately involved with child-rearing. Many of the challenges were similar for boys and girls, but in the summer of their eighth seasonal cycle, we part ways with the boys' development. They grew into men who knew their place and ensured the survival and security of the village. The girls entered training to become women and eventually village teachers. Their place was to provide sustenance, spiritual balance, ceremony and celebrations, and personal protection for the village.

Once they were called into the council circles, girls began to participate on higherlevels. They learned tribal secrets. Through the storytellers, they were offered the wisdom of their ancestors. From this age forward, the girls were expected to remember that cumulative wisdom. So by eight years of age, much of their brain patterning has been devoted to the pre-Linnaeus, native classification system, the taxonomy of plants and animals. After storytelling was added to girls' wisdom bundle, many other skills could be added over the next four seasonal rounds. They were taught to trust in their sensory awareness. They learned mapping, tanning, tracking, intuition, how to read relationships, and continuously accumulated womanhood teachings.

We draw this intimate picture of the Ancient Ones because women need a new connection. The old ways hold the many of the secrets to wholeness that modern people are seeking. In these times, an astonishing number of people are on parallel paths looking, seeking, summoning wholeness to us. We need to simply begin as the grandmothers have taught us. We need to begin in a council circle, a term I use interchangeably with women's circles. In circle, women look into each other's hearts and listen to each other's truth. Looking, listening, opening, remembering, among many, these are skills that young girls need. We will name and examine the various elements that transform a girl into a woman.

♀ ♀ ♀

Through a channel connecting to the Divine, a whispering voice of intuition, our Ancestors urge us to create beautiful, inspired work and to spend our energy on a meaningful legacy. Angeles Arrien speaks of our elders with great reverence. Now that I am an elder-becoming, I see the need for a societal path through the portal of transformation. So I look to the old ways for teachings. Grandmothers gather in a long line over my right shoulder and Grandfathers line up over my left shoulder. They watch continuously and whenever I open to new possibilities, they urge me to be brave. They inspire creativity in all of us. The old ones watch and whisper, "Will she be the one who will make a difference in the world?" In metaphorical thought, remembering our Ancestors may inspire good connections and artful work while we are here on Earth.

Earth is the place where our mission for wholeness begins. Our primal ancestors lived, in geologic terms during the Pleistocene times between 100,000 to 10,000 years ago. Before First People were displaced by agriculture and an ever progressive civilization, humans formed a relationship with the Earth and developed a perspective about where we belonged in the scheme of things. We are lucky here in North America, for less than 500 years ago our primal people were in close relationship with the Earth. Compared to the Euro-Asian perspective, we have less time to reach back over the bridge of discovery to reclaim our bond with the Earth. Within the primal people, we can still locate mentors to help us. From the rubble of the old ways, we can reclaim methods for raising the next generation to their fullest potential.

Our reclamation work depends on how successfully the older generation, now the Baby Boomers, matures and how completely we fulfill our potential. We have to reach for it, claim it and own it before we can fully understand what maturity is and how to give it away. To mentor and raise up the youngest generation, women who are elders-becoming must be realistically prepared to step up and share wisdom. Even when I don't feel so wise, I still know that all of life after fifty is a give-away.

2

Cultural Transformation of Patriarchy

I'm a woman
Phenomenally.
Phenomenal woman,
That's me.

—Maya Angelou

To become conscious cultural change agents, each woman needs to see how patriarchy has dominated her thinking. When I turned 40, awareness met me at that crossroad like the good old cosmic two by four and I realized I was lacking maturity. That's the blunt truth. I had a long financial career, but I was immature, dissatisfied and needed something else from life. What exactly was I seeking? How had I been consumed by patriarchy?

I wanted to claim maturity and I wanted it wrapped around personal knowledge, serenity, and wisdom. I needed deep connections with women who modeled maturity and would help me uncover my own. Unfortunately, in our advanced civilization and true for me at that crossroad, many millions of us miss fulfilling our highest potentials. We raise our noses from the grindstone of employment and look around, wondering where we missed maturity, wondering where our greatest potential lies hidden. Maturity may be hidden beneath "isms" like perfectionism, alcoholism, or workaholism. I merged my identity with the corporate worker and almost disappeared. How lucky for me that I began to ask those questions. It is intriguing to wonder how maturity is such a chance endeavor in these times when we're all so busy. See what your personal definition of maturity happens to be then notice how close you have come to that achievement. You may have something to celebrate or maybe the question will confront you as it did me.

To discover a defense against domination, women and girls need to delve into the nuances of patriarchy, a cultural system that is oppressive to women. This will help women defy domination and ensure long-term successes. This current social structure of patriarchal domination fails girls in two major ways. First, girls are no longer raised in Nature and, second, their three natural passages are not ceremonially celebrated. Girls need puberty rites, womanhood training and ritual initiations. Without being accepted and welcomed into the sisterhood of women, how do girls know when they have arrived? From working in the corporate world for more than twenty years, I was out of balance with womanhood. I was familiar with patriarchal power, in fact, that's what I had acquired. Once I dedicated my efforts to that work grindstone, my personal development stopped even though the job challenged me. My wholeness was temporarily suspended until I became aware that my identity was not, in fact, linked to my job. It took years of hard work to bring myself back in balance as an elder-becoming. I am still reaching for my potential, for my full maturity. Navajo culture is highly esteemed for their wisdom—their teachings say that woman's maturity happens at age fifty four. That makes good sense and will be the cause for my next celebration!

According to our current cultural model, every girl is at risk of <u>not</u> doing all the right things. The first right thing is being the good girl starting around age eleven. After that, there is a whole continuum that young women follow, at their mothers' insistence. Those steps include, becoming the best nice girl she can imagine, getting good grades, being popular and socially active, resisting sexual relationships to save her reputation, going onto a successful college experience after high school.

There are as many deviances from this scenario as there are girls. Such a continuum grew straight out of patriarchal domination, so did the image of a perfect woman's body. When girls flaunt their midriffs and bare their shoulders and legs, the male libido is being played. Flirtation is playful and good for our spirits, but falling into the cultural "norm" to please the male gender has patriarchy and low awareness intertwined.

♦ ♦ ♦

Simply put, absorption in Nature during adolescence develops brain patterning for a lifetime. From our cultural influences, real maturity remains beyond the reach of many adults. These are two reasons to look to the old ways for answers. From an imaginary bridge, we will look back to the old ways when elders were mindful of child-rearing. We will learn how they watched for wholeness and noticed shortcomings. When children are raised native to their place, deeply immersed in Nature, when they are watched and invited to stretch to wholeness, geniuses are created. I invite you to ponder these questions with me—to have full maturity by the age of 20, what are we willing to reclaim from the old ways? Are our children fulfilled? How and when do they become fully mature? Have they discovered their genius in school? What can we do to help them locate their genius?

Most modern brains lack the important scaffolding that comes from immersion in nature and full knowledge of all the plants and animals within running distance. Such scaffolding prepares human beings for any variety of challenges. I realize these are controversial claims, but remember how often you have wished for more brain power, a better memory, or the ability to grasp a difficult concept. Perhaps the neurological diseases prevalent today are preventable by simply utilizing more of our brains at an earlier age. There is so much unexplored about our brain's capabilities. While it's true that the academy and the work world challenge people's minds, neither develops the potential brain patterning nor duplicates the spiritual connection of young people to Nature. There is potentiality within both the spirit and the body. However, without training, young girls fail to develop spiritual connections with the Earth, instead they often develop phobias that can last a lifetime. We all need to recognize our presence on Earth connects us from the tiniest ant to the stars in the Milky Way. There is maturity in that humble perspective.

Human beings are the highest, most specialized life form in the animal kingdom. A full 100,000 years have passed since Homo erectus evolved into Homo sapiens, and a genome of full potential has been passed through to our genes. From birth, those genes have been endowed with "expectations" for fulfillment of a schedule of needs and abilities. When girl babies are infants, mothers are totally attentive to their needs, as dictated by their cries of hunger. Those same girls go off to school to fulfill this culture's expectations of children, namely to sit still in chairs and absorb whatever the teacher directs. Every young child has an innate curiosity for learning, kids are born natural learners. We must be careful that the restrictive structure of school does not squash their instinctive curiosity. Compare the 150 years of society's educational expectations with the hundreds of centuries of aboriginal curiosity that were satisfied simply by living close to Nature.

Even with all the scientific, intellectual and educational advances that poured over into the New Millennium, opportunities for maturity do not approach the wholeness of our genetic imprint. Immersion in Nature opens, stretches, and develops brain capacity, the vastness of knowledge amassed in our Information Age does not. Women can gather, as did our grandmothers of long ago, and teach each other ways to imprint girls to their natural environments. There are whole core curriculums now devoted to reacquainting young people with their natural environments and the skills that made our ancestors native. The easiest and most accessible skills are sitting with a quiet mind and creating a list of namable plants, trees, animals, and birds in the neighborhood. Most of us do not have the luxury of knowing pure inner silence and most people do not know their natural neighbors. Immersion in nature expands girls' brain patterning and expands their ability to locate their innate genius through constant questioning and connection to the spirit-that-lives-in-all-things. Edith Cobb reflected on her research about geniuses in Ecology of Imagination in Childhood. Her observations at playgrounds were contrasted with interviews of recognized geniuses. Edith discovered one thing about genius potential—immersion in Nature revealed one's inner genius and like a glowing ember, kept it alive.

♦ ♦ ♦

Women have the power to create a culture that is more acceptable, more cooperative and more relational for females. If all women held that intention with conscious open hearts, the circle gatherings of women and girls would change the patriarchal nature of our culture. When women learn and teach others to live relational lives, our connectedness will spread. In circles all over the country, we can diffuse the power of patriarchy and learn to gently communicate to men that we want a partnership society where dominance, brutality and physical harm become a footnote of history. In *The Chalice and the Blade*, Raine Eisler exposed the ancient cultural practices of partnership relationships with enough depth and understanding to eliminate patriarchal domination. Perhaps our greatest hope is Millennial girls will finally cause the paradigm to shift.

Some of us have arrived and have soulful partnerships while others hold the promise of that possibility in their hearts. Each of us deserves the most spiritual and equal partnerships we can imagine. Even more, a soulful partnership is one of the most desirable legacies we wish to offer the young girls we love so much.

The voluminous outpouring of women's stories and women's studies research has been testimony to how large our world might become. Already there is a long list of experiences my friends and I have known that need not be part of our daughters' lives. Those stories are pouring out of women, filling our airwaves and our bookshelves. In these changing moments, we form the bridge between the patriarchal lives of our Grandmothers and a future free of patriarchal domination. The rise of women to meet their full potential does not mean the downfall of men. Women want men to grow to their fullest potential, too. Fortunately, women are men's teachers. Since patriarchy does not serve young girls or women, a couple of small changes will make a huge difference in all our lives.

♦ ♦ ♦

The myth of "progress" we are living today does not embrace a viable or sustainable story that will move the human race into the future. As the polar opposite of sustainable, progress is harmful to all natural life on the planet. Girls' futures will be brighter if they are aware that progress is permeated with the patriarchal values of power over the earth's resources and control through force. Clear-cutting the forests and damming the rivers are ecological examples of patriarchal progress at work. At the exponential rate we have experienced for the last six decades of the 20th Century, progress will soon obliterate our planetary resources. On our current trajectory, our precious planet's resources are not sufficient to last another seven generations into the future. Many, many scholars have written about this, but they have just barely received our attention. Those seven generations are our flesh and blood. We can name them, they are our great granddaughters' great-granddaughters. Does that create a call to action inside anyone? Can the women of the world who are raising daughters bring the Earth back to a sustainable state? Together, we can create a new myth for the future that will be neither fairy tale nor fantasy. How will our story read? Ultimately, to recover a full experience of being human, we must focus on our girls when they are eight years old. An earth-based awareness will develop the potential of women and girls that will culminate in planetary restoration. Let's replace the myth of progress and create a New Story of care.

Culture's current drama makes us believe in war. We believe our military fighters are heroes, that they are warriors who struggle and conquer and overcome. We were taught by the World War generations that we should spend our lives working hard and acquiring a lot, because our worth is measured by what we own. The basic story of our consumer culture says the Earth was created for conquest and pleasure, and that the purpose of human life is to conquer and subdue the Earth. All through the 20th Century, we proved we could live without a sacred connection to Mother Nature. Our current story also emphasizes the drama of danger, cruelty and brutality—that's the story of television.

Peer into the cultural story that cuts deep into our lives and connect to how girls become women. This is the main reason girls need many women, so we can teach them how to filter the media and tune out many of the messages of power, violence, and consummerism. Growing together, women and girls can be empowered to live lives that will create change. Most of women's teaching is done by example. So what do women exemplify? Part of the transformation girls receive from their womanhood initiations is a belief in the power to change themselves and their world. In their reflection back to us, perhaps women need to quicken our own transformation. All we have to do as women gathered in small groups across the country is believe in ourselves and our own power.

Pause long enough to see the girl right in front of you. She likes her life just as it has been. Those ages ten, eleven and twelve when she created her identity have been magnificent. She has been in control and at her peak performance. Womanhood has been a curiosity point, but she does not want women's problems. As we discussed, she recognizes patriarchy, but does not accept its confinements of her freedoms, young girls refuse to accept the dominator principle of patriarchy. That's a simple denial. She hears our words about menstruation, but doesn't believe us. That's a complex denial. What girls need is a New Story that suits their development and in Millennial terms. Girls will menstruate at the early age of nine to twelve far into our human future. The way their Moon-time alters their outlook on growing into women must be considered. Most girls are not ready for womanhood at eleven or twelve. They need women to enclose them with a safe council circle to teach them why the world has changed, how to view patriarchy through a new lens, and why their bleeding is a sacred event, not dreaded or shameful.

The cultural transformations needed will be huge reasons to celebrate, so look inside with me and notice where you are now. I love ritual, it's as easy as noticing birdsong at a summer dawn or even the ritual of brushing my teeth. Ritual is a marker or a pause to notice an event in my life. When I realized that patriarchy had lost its grip on me, I opened my journal and lit a candle. I wrote for several hours about the awareness, the relief, the space that could now be filled with pure relational awareness. Such transformations require ceremony, so the many other passages in women's lives should also be considered. Initiations are meant to release life-changing losses. For girls, the loss is their girlhood, but women have journeyed far beyond their losses of childhood or girlhood. Count the other losses, such as the death of one's parents, a child or a spouse. Women roles are altered, too—daughterhood, motherhood, lover, professional. I hope other women have released the soul-robbing patriarchal grip on their lives. Life-threatening accidents, geographic moves and addictions all shatter women's confidence unless there is a ritual marker.

Whenever life-changing events move through a woman's life, she must descend into the rage, confusion, alienation, and grief. When these truths force a cleansing, a ceremony, and eventually a re-incorporation, she can sigh with relief. After that passage door is closed once again, she will notice that her maturity has been strengthened. She has been elevated, welcomed to a new normal outlook for her life.

In general, people don't give up their old story about losses, changes, developments until they are certain they will have a new story. Together, we have been imagining the grandmothers back to the time when they were called Goddesses. Even before that time, they were probably called the grandmothers. The difference between the story they lived and the story we live is a deep, wide chasm of mystery. What would we put into a New Story that would catch on like wild fire? Mothers and grandmothers of the Millennial Generation have the power to pull together a New Story about how the Earth belongs not to us, but truly, we belong to the Earth.

Women have underestimated the modeling power we have for our children. If we want to save this planet for the children of the future, then every action we take now has a direct impact. When we feel ourselves an essential part of the Nature surrounding our home, then we are native to our place. Becoming native has a place in our altered viewpoint. The domination of a power driven society is like a silent force that wishes consumers will remain alien. Nature has nothing to sell, but everything to give. By developing close relationships with every part of our natural world, we can become native again and give back to the Earth a small amount of care.

This is a choice we make. We must choose to live in alignment with Mother Earth again. We can choose to have our umbilical cord, a spiritual source of sustenance, anchored to the Earth. Wolf Hardin called this *reindigination*, that is, going deeper with our Earthly relationship and using intention as our active partner in all relationships. Through intention, we carry out plans to become intimate, to name and exchange energies with all of Nature. That is intimacy as in *into-me-see*. Allowing intimacy with our land to enter our psychic space, we will feel more at home. With a commitment to intimacy with all the natural inhabitants of the land surrounding our home, even if it's the nearest park, we grow native to our special place. A new level of comfort settles into our bones, a new sense of belonging. Attention to the details of the weather, the temperature, the sounds and smells of the seasons, distinguishes the residents from the migrants. This level of familiarity with a place causes the spirits of all the natural beings to notice us as we notice them.

Natural places provide stimulation and a serenity that speaks to my soul. I had to cut through layers of denial, but once I looked I found Nature in dense cities. There is plenty of spirit to be found within most city blocks. Birds are the most abundant wildlife in either the city or the country, and we can learn so much by watching them watch us watch them. When I give other natural beings their welcome recognition, even without speaking, I feel the response through the swaying trees, the happy-faced flowers, the soil beneath my feet, and from all the critters, every flying-crawling-leaping creature that lives with me in my place.

✦ ✦ ✦

All of humanity eventually must see itself in this story for the shift to occur. However, women can lead the way for all others. When we look deeply into our own feminine natures, we will create a new level of awareness for the feminine side of everyone. If we are brilliant, we will also see into our masculine natures. When both sides are clearly recognized, balance becomes possible. The Grandmothers, the Goddesses, knew about balance until their villages were over-run by invaders. When prehistoric women found it necessary to protect their feminine natures, the pleasant softness of being gave way to the powerful energy of doing. Agriculture all over the world was created with hefty masculine energy exerted by women, children and men. Women's perfect state of balance tipped toward a domination that has continued as a power struggle for 100 centuries.

I certainly was not raised to recognize the patriarchy in which I was immersed or to understand how it molded my early decades. Within such a patriarchal system, none of the control issues, nor the dominance were ever discussed. For inner peace and well-being, children need to develop and become intimate with their inner energies, their feminine energy of being that needs quiet and nurturance and masculine energy of doing that needs to see progress, wants to get things completed. The time to raise girls' awareness of balance between these two inner energies is when they are emerging from the dreamy state of early childhood to the more thoughtful late childhood years. As we develop our New Story together, circles will offer comprehensive training for girls' needs, for understanding patriarchal dominance, for dialoguing with women about what they most want to know, and innumerable other subjects. Since the media has exposed even the most personal subjects, girls can enjoy open discussions in the safety of their women's circles.

We are conscious, spiritual, reflective beings capable of living with simplicity, elegance, and deeply caring for the Earth, our beloved relation. Our new story is a story of belonging and expresses itself through relationships. We come to learn the meaning of love through quiet personal reflection, through what Nature offers to teach us and through raising our current awareness to successive levels. We learn that all of life is divine and love is life in divine consciousness.

Modern culture has taught women to hide our true selves. This has been a direct result from the effects of patriarchy on our adolescent years. I learned this from Carol Gilligan, but all of the girls in my programs have proved it to be a truth. See how this is true for you. In a multitude of ways, we mask the magnificence of our being-ness to protect ourselves. Part of the self has been hidden for survival—a survival that means something different than it did before modern times. Today, in addition to survival meaning "not to die," it also means to endure, sustain, persist, exist, withstand, be brave, and persevere. These descriptors express the essence of many contemporary women and all contemporary adolescent girls. After all of women's victories, survival in contemporary culture still means the maintenance of primarily masculine relationships.

The patriarchy of domination that permeates society is only part of the reason for the silence of females. Adolescent girls also find it psychologically necessary to resist many parts of modern womanhood. Girls' resistance is an expression of their struggle for personal power in a world where power is stripped from the less forceful gender and hoarded through control and money. When women's voices are hushed unwillingly, when our sparkle and liveliness need to be shielded from view, our spirit-self knows that existence is the equivalent of dying. If this seems extreme to you, look carefully around your circle to gently help your friends transform domination. Girls who were hushed grew into women who are meek, over-polite, and work very hard to please every soul. Being hushed too much means they must be "good girls" more than they wish, and their opinions are devalued. That is the womanhood girls resist.

We are women and our natures strive for balance and harmony. However, in most places on the planet, our balancing and harmonizing spirits have yielded to the dominant forces of thousands of years of patriarchy. In this culture, we can reclaim our true natures, but we just need to know how. For many who have discovered equal and spiritual partnerships, survival has evolved into thriving. From an ecological worldview, two perspectives become obvious. Domination has long manipulated women and the planet. The earth needs our brilliant awareness and our spirits need to finally rise above the power and control of patriarchy. For peace and harmony to reign free, it must be true all around the globe. That means we begin at home and build model partnerships. I respectfully direct your curiosity to the workbook by Raine Eisler and her partner David Loye, *The Partnership Way: New Tools for Living and Learning*. They have clearly defined the dualism between dominator and partnership relationships. Women deserve to have this awareness in our bundle of knowledge. We deserve to be women free from fears or doubts about our place, about our essence and about how to achieve balance and harmony.

♀ ♀ ♀

Looking forward to the unfolding of the ancient wisdom of womanhood, we will review our needs from memory. Our contemporary preadolescent girls and pre-adult young women would surely like to know there are developmental choices available. They want to hear of a different way, an ancient way that comes through nature and mentoring. Can we shift to a New Story if girls intentionally and gently place one foot in a naturalist culture created around their women's circle and leave one foot in their pop culture until they mature? True to a social experiment, this straddle will offer girls so many more choices for their maturity than contemporary culture now offers without the shock of a complete change. Women will form a circle group around their girls and simultaneously demonstrate the many faceted women's roles of mother, nurturer, provider, leader, networker, healer and lover of all of life.

Without such a circle filled with role models, our contemporary adolescents fall short of feeling grounded in being-ness or in having a sense of
belonging. Each girl needs the guidance of many women to sink one
foot in each of the two cultural worlds, the natural world and the contemporary culture. Planning and preparation for girls' Rites of Passage
into womanhood will provide girls motivation for demonstrating skills
earned from a challenge. With planning, every intention is possible in a
women's group, even creating the time to choreograph and perform a
Rite of Passage for each young woman. With ceremony to celebrate her
womanhood, each adolescent girl will enter her womanhood blossom
free of detached or wounded attitudes. Fortunate for women, our
remembering is cumulative. Our girls will benefit from all our discoveries.

We have an opportunity to understand the different characteristics
from matrilineal cultures that could easily be incorporated into our lives.
As a woman, you can respond to your ancestors' questions and reach out
for a new level of maturity, as your search rewards you with a new level
of awareness. For you and your relations, each level of maturity makes a
difference. Rites of Passage for adolescents, elder mentoring for young
adults, and every possible opportunity to raise the next generation to its
full potential will make the culture more tolerable and the world more
livable. Paul Shepard, reminded us in *Coming Home to the Pleistocene*,
"We humans are instinctive culture makers; given the pieces, the culture
will reshape itself."

3

Girls' Needs

Circle Invocation Excerpt

For there is vulnerability, fear, love, rage, hatred,
compassion, courage, despair, and hope
In ourselves, each other, and the world.
May we know our most authentic feelings
And voice them when we speak.
May we form and become a circle.
Begin by holding hands in a circle
Be silent and feel the clasp and connection
Of hands and heart.
Then each in turn
Speak for yourself
And listen to each other.
Put judgment aside
Sing what spontaneously wants to be sung.
And end each circle as it was begun.
Invite blessings.
Until we meet again.

—Jean Shinoda Bolen

♀ ♀ ♀

What precisely do eight-year-old girls need? Or girls who are eleven or fifteen, how have their needs changed? We begin with age eight, the year that introduces a developmental stage known as Late Childhood. We must proceed cautiously, knowing that change will naturally evolve in each girl. At eight, girls still have an attachment to the wonderful comfort they experienced throughout their early childhood—a phase marked by a vast absorption of information, by delirious play accompanied by almost constant laughter, by an awakened imagination and by significantly expanded thinking abilities.

As they approach their ninth birthday, girls will pull themselves up and out of their child-magnet ever so gradually. Their minds and bodies will do sufficient pushing, so all we need to do is greet them with a new awareness. Imagine a bridge. On it, women and girls meet in a magical place known as *womanhood training grounds*. Although these girls are still a long way from womanhood, soon we will notice they have only one foot left in childhood. Around age ten just when nobody is looking, they will move onto a threshold. Both feet will be planted firmly at the doorway of womanhood. From there they will look around, put their hands on their hips, swing from one foot to the other and ask, "Has anybody noticed how much I've changed?"

Along the developmental continuum, different needs arise at different ages. The needs of an eight-year-old girl are quite different than those of a one-year-old girl. Both need love, family and a safe environment that includes shelter and good, healthy food. Both have rapidly expanding brains and bodies and need to explore their world with age-appropriate safety. The grandmothers of long ago recognized other changes in the eight-year-old mind, body and spirit. They saw that a passage was opening, which we now call late childhood. Modern mothers of eight-year-olds can breathe a sigh of relief, their daughters are still little girls for a while longer. However, the girls' worldview has expanded much more than you realize. Age eight to nine their invisible antennas grow. Girls watch women with an ever-growing intensity.

Biological changes happen on an individual clock, with each passing month, women role models become increasingly important.

The year between eight and nine is the age that female hormones are released into the blood stream. Girls suddenly need much more information from women about the changes in their little bodies. Today, hardly anyone teaches the young people about their inner terrains. Girls need to become conversant about all of their hormones, like the vital one, cortisol, that directs our response to stress. All the other hormones cause interesting consequences, also. Shouldn't we explain to girls how they have both masculine and feminine strengths and identities? They have hormones that are female, primarily estrogen. One of the lessons for our daughters will be how to identify their animus energy, the tough, assertive, get-it-done energy controlled by the testosterone hormone which every woman has along with estrogen.

If you've been watching, mother and grandmother, you almost saw her passage doorway swing open. The passage from early childhood to late childhood is the first of three passages that girls grow through before they fly from the nest. In the old days, women gathered in small circles with their eight-year-old girls. The monthly gathering circle was the girls' first step along the way to their coming of age ceremony. Regularly, they practiced womanhood rituals, they asked and answered thousands of questions in the safety of small numbers and they planned challenges woven around nature celebrations such as Solstice and Equinox. Eventually, the whole village celebrated each girl's passage to adulthood.

How did mothers train daughters for womanhood way back in those simpler times when whole circles of women helped each girl come into her fullest bloom? Throughout the 20th Century, women won successive victories over history to finally allow her-stories to be heard. Because of our proven ability to express her-stories in the making, I know women have the ability to create a new culture for girls. All the needs presented here are best discussed in women's council circles. Imagine girls' delight when they are placed center stage for a day each month. As months roll by, girls will push their way into puberty.

Around age eleven or perhaps even twelve or thirteen, the portal to womanhood finally opens. Mothers and mentors have much more responsibility for these girls than was ever imagined in prehistory. Puberty, the middle passage, is marked by physical changes, both visible and invisible. Spiritual, mental and emotional changes can be as dramatic as the bodily changes. Through awareness and thoughtfulness, all of girls' changes will become visible enough to be celebrated.

The important piece I discovered in my doctoral research is how biologically different Millennium girls are from girls just five or six generations ago. Physical development has a profound effect on spirituality, psyche, and personal perception. All around the globe, girls develop both sooner and faster. Menstrual cycles come as early as nine or ten, while today's norm is age twelve. For the thousands of years prior to 1900, girl's normal menstrual time was around sixteen years old. That shocking fact raises so many questions. A hundred years ago, the timing of girls' first Moon cycle began changing. Physicians I queried about this phenomenon led me to research nutrition. Our nutrition is now continuously available and generally of consistent quality. Regarding animal protein consumption, one of the big questions concerns what the animals are fed. Have the diets of farm animals been supplemented with hormones or antibiotics? Back in our ancestral lineages, there were times of abundance, to be sure, but there were also times of scarcity. Most of the differences can be attributed to this phenomenal combination—the absence of feast and famine in our diets and the quality of animal protein.

Girls are not ready for full womanhood status at age twelve, nor should they be. Like the undressing of deciduous trees for winter, our genes maintain a reliable developmental continuum. In daily life and through formal challenges, girls need to have their important stages noticed and celebrated. Girls need to be welcomed by women through each of their passage portals. I believe the ceremony that coincides with her first moon, the initial cycle marked by a girl's first bleeding, should be celebrated as Puberty Rites. Then womanhood initiation ceremonies should be observed sometime later when her full bloom of womanhood bursts open. At both puberty and womanhood ceremonies, girls need to be welcomed as women. However, at puberty, girls need to know there is much they still have to learn, their womanhood welcome is for their first step along the path to womanhood. In contrast, at an initiation ceremony, a Rites of Passage, a young woman is ready to stand independent, while embracing interdependence.

Depending on the circle of women who support each girl's training, their monthly gatherings will be unique. An accumulation of circumstances, challenges, blessings and trials must be designed for each girl. Starting here, starting now, we should amass the wisdom needed to recreate ritual traditions like our grandmothers of old. However, our wisdom and ritual traditions need to be contemporary, they are essential parts to the New Story that fits with our times. This will pull young girls into their next stage of development with notable wholeness. Scientifically, this is called ontogeny.

♀ ♀ ♀

It's essential to understand that we were raised to the best of our mothers' abilities, but unfortunately, in most cultures, it's been generations since initiation ceremonies were offered to girls coming of age. African Americans, Apaches, Navajos, Plains Indians, Ojibwas and a few other cultures have small circles of women who tightly hold their ceremonial threads or they have worked to reclaim their ancestors' wisdom before it was completely lost. Only a few lucky girls are offered the whole of womanhood before they fly free of their mother's nest. We are now re-inventing what has been lost for many years.

I have consulted a plethora of reference materials and offer a bit of that to you here. Immersed in my research, I could hear the tiny voice of wisdom inside which seems so simple, but it feels urgent to me. It is about creating a New Story for womanhood in this new Century, this new Millennium. To mothers, grandmothers, mentors, muses, I say this: Just do it! Begin with a circle of committed women who will surround your precious girls. Meet once a month for her years between ages eight and eighteen—put the date in glowing colors on your busy schedules! Circles and ceremonies are what each girl needs most. In fact, wrapped together in one bundle, that would be about all she really needs. If you meet regularly with her and a group of girls who will grow to be lifelong friends, you will find laughter, healing, balance, harmony, empowerment, skills, self-esteem, confidence, spirit, wholeness and many other things. One short generation of women's circles for girls and there would be no more holes in women's power centers.

When girls pass through their Puberty Rites and into their middle and late teen years, their needs do not stop expanding. Girls need community and challenges. They need to exert full control over their bodily experience, who they see in the mirror, their sexual desires, their nutrition and exercise. Girls need experiences that will increase their self-worth. Community service projects are one avenue available to girls. Others include school activities, random acts of kindness, helping others, career shadowing and jobs.

Girls need to raise their awareness to guard against their peers' view of deviance, a label girls might receive if they are not with a man. In the sexual arena, girls' bodies force them to be good managers, for they must not be so flirtatious as to attract criticism but flirtatious enough to gain a man's attention. For very fortunate girls, circles of committed women will stick with them and notice their needs. Girls who dance free of the nest after a decade of women's circles will not feel they have been betrayed, because they will have enough information and sense of self to navigate in the world.

Girls need the trusted connection to mothers, mentors, peers and friends who are intimates in their circle where their voices can be heard. So much drama happens to adolescent girls. Women within their trusted circle could direct girls out of their self-centered drama and into skills building. In addition to the long topic-lists on womanhood, middle and late adolescent girls want to question women on sex, pregnancy, body image, sexual harassment, peer pressure, prejudice, drugs, loneliness, sisterhood and more. These are topics that dare women to tell the truth and feel acceptance for their views, their experiences and their courage to speak from their hearts.

All through her teen years, your daughter needs encouragement to articulate her life. Many steps go into the making of a woman. Our genetic blueprint is so keen, we know the developing mind-body-spirit cannot be stopped. However, girls need their unconscious development to be brought into their conscious awareness.

♦ ♦ ♦

Let's introduce the future. Beginning at age eight, each girl wants and needs to know in advance that changes are coming. Gentle discussions about where girlhood and womanhood separate—your girl's first Moon bleeding—will be most helpful if introduced positively. If girls have this discussion with their friends before their parents, much of the positive potential may be lost. Each girl needs to know that whenever she has her Moon cycle, a sacred door opens in her spirit. She is most creative and introspective during this special time of the month. Each young girl needs to know she carries the power to give birth to another in her long and special ancestral lineage, and she must use that power with full awareness.

Particularly in this Western culture, our foremothers in the 20th Century dreaded even one conversation about girls' menstrual cycles. Sadly, women must admit our mothers passed down hesitancy and, yes, fear, and it's time to break out of that fear. Like Gloria Steinem, I came from the "down there" generation. The women in my life avoided any mention of down there or what makes us women or the differences between the sexes. It's a mystery how menses, body changes and sexuality became the hardest of all discussion topics for women. We are fortunate that all that has finally changed. The last of those old taboos have been lifted by television and computer exposure. The sphere of sexuality is so out in the open now, girls become conversant through emerging relationships with peers at a very young age, as early as eight. With the rise of feminism, the women's movement and the media, so much is available to girls that mothers need to have Moon-time conversations when girls are eight, then again at nine and ten. Girls will be excited to know a power and a privilege will accompany her Moon-time. A woman's spiritual doorway swings open on her first Moon and with awareness, can be built into a powerful spiritual experience she glories in each month. Awareness and preparation are the keys to changing the paradigm from what we have known to a whole new way for young girls coming up.

As women create a New Story to be handed down to daughters, we need to blend back in the sacred nature of ourselves. Month after month, menses signals an opening of our women's spirits. Women who are aware of their place in the cosmos have a spiritual connection to their creativity. From the precious, ancient genome, each monthly cycle signals an opportunity to focus and further develop our womanly spirituality and our connection to the Divine Feminine. To dissolve the last of the hesitation and fear, we must reintroduce the feminine as our sacred domain. We must remind each girl that sexual experience is gathered over a lifetime. Mothers, grandmothers and mentors need to lead those intimate conversations because women's ability to create new life is in a web with the survival of all other species on this planet, indeed the planet herself. As Judy Grahn said in *How Menstruation Created the World*, "It followed that *women's* logic must lie at the base of menstrual rituals." Like an ever-enlarging spiral, intimacy and sexuality are core subjects from which all others spin. In circles with young girls, women all over the country will be re-creating the gentlest, sacred rituals for their daughters' menses, and will lead to womanhood's New Story.

† † †

I call this section, sex at ten, or was that twelve? Women have underestimated a new Millennium sex craze that has swept through our schools and communities. To illustrate the delicacy of oral sex between very young boys and girls, Oprah Winfrey and Phil McGraw have both aired shows this year, 2004. With every aim-to-please and relationship gene they possess, girls are allowing boys to take advantage of them for oral sex. Most parents, teachers and social workers are in denial about what is happening at home, in dark corners, or at the back of the bus. Blend girls' intense desire for relationships with a dare or with a bit of defiance, and boys can talk girls into anything. The new craze is about the five full minutes it takes a girl to give oral sex to a boy—five minutes anywhere and everywhere. The most dangerous fuel for this fire is mothers' denial—"Not my daughter" or "I have a very close relationship with my daughter, she would never…"

Yes, she would, Mother. She would do just about anything for close relationships, so we need to focus on what girls need and women's awareness of those needs. Girls need frank discussions in closed and safe circles about how to develop a sacred-self image, about natural sexual desires, and on how to build relationships out of love and trust. We could assemble an astute panel of psychologists and sociologists to discuss the consequences. Each girl's moral and social reasoning might be just a little different. Let's not judge girls for wanting prestige, power, fun, or relationships. For their self-image and self-esteem, women can surround girls with women's circles and reconnect to the Divine Feminine. This craze can be just that, a short lived fad. But let's remain in a proactive mode, the next craze may shock us even more.

Mothering is not only an instinct, it's also a daring adventure. Look inside to when you were ten, and you'll see your girl. This is the age relationship-making rises to top priority. Their relationship with you receives top billing, too. Girls feel a need to copy your every move, but you can rest assured this is a phase, even though it is somewhat intimidating. Copying can last three or more years and is important for many reasons. Her intentional conditioning comes from these years of increasing awareness. This means we will always be like the woman who mothered us. We become individuated through the strength of our wills. If a girl is extremely fortunate, there will be many women nearby who model womanhood and who weave themselves into her sphere of experience. Pam Schiller said, "Experience is the architect of the brain."

More than formal education, girls' brain patterning is designed by experiences.

Women have the gifts and characteristics that girls need, women are receptive, nurturing and relational. We have what they are seeking. Watch girls watching women. They want the details to seep into the marrow of their young bones—every inner feminine detail which dances with every masculine detail of her animus. The anima is the personification of all feminine psychological tendencies within a man. Anima is the archetypal feminine symbolism within a man's unconscious, as seen in men who are gentle, tender, patient and receptive. The animus is the personification of all masculine psychological tendencies within a woman. Animus is the archetypal masculine symbolism within a woman's unconscious, we can be assertive, controlling, with an inner warrior, and take charge of things. Girls are sponges who notice every little thing, like how we blend our energies or our ability to *be* (feminine) and our ability to *do* (masculine) anything we create with our heart-minds. Inside of our experience and knowledge, we hold what they most desire—the wisdom to help them gain experience. We know it and they know it. Allow the girls to be like keys, to slip into your heart and find ways to unlock those Divine Feminine secrets.

♀ ♀ ♀

Girls' basic needs are bare necessities. Many millions of young girls spend their whole lives concerned with the most basic of needs. In this country, several hundred thousand children are homeless right now. Shelter and food form the foundation of needs, though they are quite distinctive needs. For those fortunate enough to have shelter, some girls might be sharing a bedroom with younger boy siblings. At this age, that requires a rearrangement. Girls are fine sharing a bedroom, even a bed, with sisters, but at age eight, a separation between boys and girls is necessary.

Food is another matter altogether. Preferences and habits begin very young, so tutor girls about both nutrition and choice. Food will be an enduring "best topic" to discuss in circles. At times, everyone's diet needs a thorough review. A refresher course in nutrition opens a line of communication between mothers and daughters. Food and nutrition are so personal, media should not influence our decisions.

In circles, one of the nutrition topics should be conventional or organic food choices, including the issue of genetically modified foods. Young girls don't realize they are the first generation to be impacted by corporate alteration of a food's basic genes. Even the four food groups are no longer stable as we once imagined, and breakthrough discoveries continually challenge our ability to stay current. The basics are just a way to develop an understanding and to question the validity of your core beliefs. Begin with a new emphasis on fresh and organic foods. Children are allowed far too many sodas, sweets and refined carbohydrates. To build on their experience, girls need to begin food preparations and nutritional awareness. Women can organize pot luck lunches for their day in circle and the girls can make special dishes to share with their mentors and friends as a creative adventure from their kitchen. Girls need to be taught early that, "You are what you eat." It is one powerful way to teach choices.

Beyond food and shelter, girls need each other. I pause here to emphasize this. For a few moments, be still and reflective about your own late childhood years. What did you need back then? We still cherish camp memories with special friends, sleepovers with neighbors and classmates, and all the memories when girls and women gathered close together. Decades later, we still feel wonderment for how all those things remain alive in our heart-minds. What was missing in your own experiences? Your answer is key to how you move through your daughters' adolescent years. Women need to provide girls with the fond memories of experiences we did get and also what we didn't get and still miss. Perhaps the most healing of all question-answer meditations is, "Based on my wisdom now, what did I need when I was her age?" Make your own personal list of needs. Women and girls have all the same needs, just different times and intensities.

Girls have a need to be social, so friends become increasingly important to them. The bonds of friendship are the first indicators in a long
process of separation from the bonds of family. Girls need to enter relationships with their friends with an awareness of the spiritual formula
of giving and receiving. This formula will serve them through their
whole lives and through innumerable relationships. A bit of elaboration
may be helpful. Each girl-to-girl connection can be positive if it's made
with awareness. Girls require a little tutoring about relationships, about
their sacred nature, and about how the mind inside their heart stirs their
connection into a lasting bond. Friends become friends through an
attention-response system that is mostly unspoken. They give and we
receive in some proportion that creates balance. Then, we give and they
receive. Sometimes friends are mirrors for sensibilities that feel warm to
our hearts, so contact with friends feels safe. To build relationships that
are deep and true to our individual growth and development, girls need
time to nurture friendships, just as we do.

One of the ways girls can be taught to build good strong relationships is learning that we are all related. When girls are taught to be
thoughtful, reverent and careful with nature, that kindness can be trans-
ferred toward their friends as well as other people. Place a nature
baby—kitten, puppy, colt or kid—near a young girl, give her space and
then watch what happens. When she elaborates on the experience,
encourage her to speak with all of her senses. That same tenderness,
once it is spoken with her full awareness, will also become available to
her friends. This is another powerful way to teach about choices.
Friends are among the most important choices made in life at all ages.

† † †

What advice do we give the pre-adolescent or adolescent girl who
looks up with adoring eyes and is all ears for our next morsel of wisdom?
My advice is that you have courage, mothers and grandmothers, to be
all you can be. Take your first step with courage and the next one with
intention. We are role models, so let's be brilliant. The roles around any

intentional circle cover the needs of women and girls. What is needed for wholeness? Skills, stories, leadership, and creative expression are the roles women model in life, build your circle around those roles.

If we can learn stories to share with our daughters and their friends, perhaps the *Othermothers*—all those other women who help mother your daughter—will do the same. Othermothers are part of our extended families and have a relationship with a girl's mother so that they can act as a bridge to a fresh perspective. They may also come right off the pages of our favorite myths. Othermothers are part of the community; they are aunts, older sisters, family friends, cousins. Othermothers make certain to communicate to girls that they are special. Psychically, Othermothers can "be there" for girls in ways that mothers are not allowed. Being trusted and respected by mothers, Othermothers create a safe, tight weave around the girls.

The Grandmothers have always offered memories through shared stories, parables, myths, fairy tales and new stories. Honor your Elders by passing on an abundance of their teaching stories—if not from your own grandmothers, then from your general heritage. There are references in Appendix A to guide you and please allow your own curiosity to expand this list.

In addition to published stories, women have thousands of personal stories and your circles will create more. As this New Story for Womanhood unfolds, our web site, www.womenmentoringgirls.org will have a network through which girls can share their stories with each other. Girls will receive a citation credit for every story and every photo they submit. All girls are encouraged to explain how they won new skills, to share the secret within a fabulous dish they offered to their circle, and the stories of their Puberty Rituals and Rites of Passage ceremonies. This will be a part of Womanhood's New Story as we work to re-create our culture together. Parables, myths and stories support a metaphorical way of transferring knowledge, and it is the oldest way of sharing wisdom with young girls. Their upturned faces are eager for everything women have to share. After puberty, we give them the story books, turn the tables on them and they learn to be the storytellers. Although many parents do enjoy reading with their children, the art of storytelling can be spun into reading activities. When girls learn to entertain by memorizing short parables and myths, everyone learns. In *Women Who Run With The Wolves*, Clarissa Estés shares a discussion of her stories that teach how to squeeze the wisdom out of the myth and parables. It's a way of analyzing events that will carry over into the dramas of our lives, so lessons can be absorbed through stories. Our lives contain many of the same dramas we find in the parables and heroine stories. *Her-stories* do repeat century to century with twists and turns of the times.

*   *   *

Each girl holds her own stories, and those stories must be told. She must tell them herself and she favors any forum where she has good listeners. We should never underestimate this need of each girl to mold and retell the events of her life, for it is one of the major means of prevention of risks for all of womanhood. We never stop needing to be heard. Better than a prescription for therapy, women's narratives have continual therapeutic results. When we tell our stories to eager listeners, we become the best parts again and again. We are each a collective of experiential stories that we can hardly wait to share. Stories heard in a receptive environment encourage adventures. We want to make more stories so interesting that they can be told over and over. When we open our hearts to a group of trusted listeners, we often have the opportunity to hear ourselves think. New matters are synthesized, as the space between our hearts and our brains grows into one continuous channel.

Sometimes a story requires courage to get the truth out. Courage is crucial to living a full and abundant life. Girls definitely need courage and need to watch women with courage. How women operate in our lives absorbs into their young bones as if through direct osmosis. However, in spite of our encouragement to be brave, much of living is stopped because of fear. All kinds of fear stops us: fear of failure, fear of success, fear of what people will think or say and fear of feeling all of our emotions. The fear of fully experiencing love stops too many from having what they most desire. Have the courage to live. Taking a risk on living—instead of avoiding living—is the only way to reach for the brass rings. If we want the prize, the brass rings representing our hearts' desire, we must risk something of ourselves. This subject of courage is close to my heart. I have had and lost courage many times. Certainly, all the moments, days, weeks I lived in fear were lessons. Once I became acquainted with the depths of my shadow-side, I learned that wallowing there only engenders more regrets. The light I reach for is vast if it is equal to the shadow I have known. The number of days I spent wallowing barely enter my consciousness now. The light side of my life is so dear and the courage to stay here on the edge reinforces itself over and over. Knowing all that comes through lessons—even what are often called mistakes—I choose to live life with courage. We can each choose to co-create our lives with courage in order to be all that our potentials hold.

Courage is one of the topics to be visited over and over in a myriad of ways within your circle. When women hold courage up as a virtue, girls will understand that is how to make their dreams come true. All dreams deserve support, but I have found that girls hesitate to speak in terms of what they intend to do in their lives. So, wrapped in the bundle with courage is the freedom to dream. To propel dreams into the future, to make them come true, girls need to be spiritually trained to use their intentions.

♦ ♦ ♦

When women call a circle, their whole heart needs to be in the mix. The calling of a circle is a rather serious matter. While there is a large element of playfulness, the underlying commitment is serious. A circle in which young girls are invited to participate is so ancient, they will respond with enthusiasm. Girls' ancestral genes have anticipated the invitation. However, please understand that girls become expectant rather quickly. When something is this special, all women relish the heightened anticipation and expect its magic to go on forever. That's what circles will be for girls, so make certain the commitment is do-able. If need be, build in flexibility. With flexibility, we don't have to work so hard to forgive when one or two women have something unexpected come up. Sometimes girls may have to be present without their mothers, so make that acceptable from the beginning. Sometimes mothers may even be present without their daughters, so make that acceptable also.

Women need to be the instigators to start circles for any age of girls, but the recommendation is to begin when girls are eight years old. This is the ideal age to design a positive path to Puberty Rites and beyond. When mothers, grandmothers and othermothers begin the whispering, girls' curiosities soar. They know when something's afoot. Remember, their little invisible antennae's have emerged. As a woman-becoming, their senses have awakened out of the dreamy stage of childhood. Let them know that something is being stirred, planned for them and watch their desire level rise. Create the longing and encourage them to remember that gathering with women is an ancient need.

Women readers will have girls who represent all the ages between eight to eighteen. Begin where you are together. Girls who are twelve and older have more of life's experience to share; perhaps they have encountered the patriarchal wall and need strong, clear women's role models more than ever. Women are instigating what, precisely? The answer is deep and perhaps somewhat academic. Women will be helping girls develop brain patterning to supplement formal education. Women will be creating a safety net for prevention. What needs preventing? A ritual womanhood training may prevent any number of things (see the Risk List in Appendix B), but primary mother/daughter and womanhood wounds are significant. Emotional losses are almost unavoidable, but resiliency can evolve from losses. Early pregnancy is at the top of the prevention list, as well as runaways, loss of communication, eating disorders and teen sex. Mothers, grandmothers, look at your relationship right now, but please don't go into denial. "Not my daughter," or "We're too close." Those simple denials produce millions of stories about regrets. Later in life, any one of us may say, "I wish I would have..."

Imagine a circle of women and girls after a year of meetings. That is a technique known as *thinking from the end*. Speak to other women to decide on a group size, on meeting times and on the level of ritual. Since we are coming together to create this New Story for womanhood, no one gets to be rule maker alone. The nicest circles have a few rules created by the group and a shared leadership. Women's circles have little or no room for finger-pointing or advice or judgments, just experiential stories that begin, "Here's what happened to me."

Girls programs are quite successful with an age appropriate mix (8–11, 12–15, and 16–18) but that is not a rule. Perhaps the month to month flow of the circle could be based on fulfilling the needs of the group. Successful circles depend on women's willingness to respond to girls' needs. At what level are mothers, grandmothers and mentors willing to commit? Women may need to meet a few times, perhaps as many as six or eight times, to feel sure about their mission. It would be a good idea to even create a vision statement so the circle holds a power of its own. If the ancient ways were re-enacted, monthly circles would be called to share a way of being. The commitment is the most important part of this planning. After all, a committed gathering of women with girls has taken care of itself for thousands and thousands of years. Current culture prevails, so to overlay something primal that is so new to many may require us to be our fluid best. We may need to schedule way ahead, even a year or more. First or fourth Saturdays or second or third Sundays may work for some groups. Other groups may choose the organic rhythm of the moon, either the new Moon or the full moon, but remember the home fires. There may be husbands, boy children, even babies to be cared for if women and girls separate for this day. This commitment needs to go deep, very deep.

When a circle is called, a new level of awareness enters the spirit of all who participate. That awareness floats on the wind and hums through the treetops. It is a belonging. All people love and need to belong, being a member of a circle resonates from the most ancient genetic code we carry. Women's circles are for womanhood's maturity. Circles will reveal the most sacred and the most mundane features of our lives and raise both to a level of celebration. Circles do not have to be planned to the nth degree, the vibrancy from a circle relies on women's commitment to share womanhood with girls and to fulfill the most basic of needs. These needs are the need to belong, the need to feel a part of the whole and the need to be celebrated as passages open. In circles that begin when girls are age eight, three passages will naturally occur. The first is also the most subtle, girls shed their early childhood with barely a whimper. They enter a mock-grown-up phase, a mimic time when they watch and directly copy women's behaviors. Entering the second passage, girls drop childhood and embrace puberty. Girls exaggerate the mimicry of all women, they become skilled chameleons and try on the most outrageous behaviors they see. Know that the whole world is their oyster; wide exposure is as good for girls as well defined boundaries. Their enthusiasm may be deflated by the patriarchal wall, be watchful for voices that succumb to "I don't know." Girls need to be stretched, challenged, and tested to approach their full bloom. Her last passage comes to her like the brass ring, she's reached for it, she's worked hard, all the women in the circle agree womanhood belongs to her. Each girl, one by one, will be called to her past passage and a well planned choreography should be waiting for them. Women will notice all these passages on the path to womanhood because they are watching the girls very carefully. Much of what evolves in circles is about changes that rely on spirit, because they are unforeseen. Circle time will be set aside for the observation and celebration of the natural events in women's lives.

♀ ♀ ♀

In New York, Krista Oracea looked inside her experience and discovered a formula for her eight-year-old daughter. By stretching the boundaries of her community and forming a committed circle with the mothers of other girls, women gather under a group promise to share wisdom with their daughters. They meet by consensus, when all the women and girls say yes. They don't need to have a ten-year agenda, for they are organic and fluid. All together, they trust that the developmental needs of the girls will show them their way into womanhood. Women's wisdom knows the way. An Elder or Auntie escorts one of the girls if her mother is truly stuck with dueling priorities.

Imagine the intricate web of women's experience these girls will have with each other and with their mothers, mentors, and othermothers after a decade of such gatherings. The girls have been placed on a sacred pedestal, showing them they are special enough to deserve time away with women. In mathematical terms, it's one hundred and twenty days, a four-month experience stretched into a decade filled with awe, anticipation, ceremony, celebrations, and the graceful flexibility of women's humor and wisdom. I support this sacred gathering, I applaud it, and I know the ancestral Grandmothers have whispered in Krista's ear. Although I have searched, I haven't found another circle begun at the portal of Late Childhood. Oh, how I hope there are other circles for girls who have begun early and now have stories to share. Many womanhood circles for girls are essential to our New Story and they are key to finding a new way to nurture and protect our daughters.

Inside a formal council circle, a small group of women, say six or eight, can share with their daughters. The number is not fixed by anyone. There may be more women sometimes, more girls other times. Circles require a level of commitment that is both firm and fluid. Say the circle agrees to meet once a month, maybe on the third Saturday or on each full moon, that's a rigorous and serious commitment. A flexibility that allows for an occasional absence promotes complete forgiveness by others in the circle. Serious also means inclusivity and diversity with a range of ages. Elders are especially valuable role models for eight to eighteen year old girls.

A council circle needs to be honored for its own energy, and once started, it should continue until the last daughter has been prepared to fly free and has ceremoniously celebrated her departure for college or work away from home. Since such a circle is for women's spiritual work, women may continue to meet, celebrated and departed young women still occasionally drop by. Such a projection takes us so far into the future, we can barely go there in our imaginations. Evolvement should occur—the circle might be re-opened any time for make room for new girls.

Two or more mothers need to get the circle started by looking at their girls' friends and deciding who should be included. Think carefully about the age span. This is a rather serious consideration because of the sacred subject—womanhood—and because each female has unique gifts to offer the other circle participants. Circles become community places to share each woman's gifts and lessons. Be flexible and patient in the dynamics of the circle, don't rush to close the circle to new members too soon. You might want to invite two elders, a daughter-less mother or even a creative muse. Leave your circle open for a few meetings to be sure about the members. Announce ahead of time when the circle will close. Closing a circle creates a safe, secure vessel for everyone. Remember a circle is not a place for power struggles, but rather a place to celebrate women's power. If you feel you need more definition about circles before you are ready to venture on your own, I recommend PeerCircles authored by Christine Baldwin (*Calling the Circle : The First and Future Culture*) as a guide for shared leadership and longevity. My own circle mentor is Jean Shinoda Bolen, author of *The Millionth Circle: How to Change Ourselves and The World—The Essential Guide to Women's Circles.* She promotes women's circles world-wide based on the hundredth monkey principal. Simply because a hundred monkeys went to the stream to wash their yams, all monkeys now wash their yams in the nearest water. Because circles fill such an ancient need to teach womanhood to girls, circles will spread around the world and gradually change our patriarchal world just like the hundred monkeys going to the stream.

What happens in a women's circle when women include their young daughters? Some mothers are sensitive to what their girls are exposed to, so boundaries and limits need to be discussed in the women's planning group before daughters are invited. For example, sexual discussions may demand age appropriateness, a topic to be defined by the women. A circle of women and girls can form organically—mothers may get acquainted in their third grader's classrooms. Once a circle is formed, women who gather regularly to talk, laugh, celebrate and cry for joy, will find it difficult to imagine life without a circle. But, it is more than that. It is a woman telling all the other women the truth of what is really going on in her inner life, her spiritual life and her outer life. Any fear that arises will be dissolved by the love and trust felt in the circle. Have patience, this circle is essential for women's growth as much as for girls' growth. Many issues naturally will come along and fill the space—planned celebrations of one of the girl's passages, honoring of one of the elders, or just the sharing and processing of life together. Outer themes like community or political issues may creep in, or inner issues like nutrition, health or beliefs may rise to the surface. Women are so complex, there will never be a shortage of topics.

A woman's circle is free space, a vessel in which you can be yourself. You can start a circle and think it's going to be wonderful, then, whoops, there are bumps and even shadow problems. If a drama or a crisis happens, the strength of women will be revealed. Consult with your elders and each other, then go dig in the Earth for guidance. The circle can be a container for growth and transformation. Be glad we don't have to remain caterpillars forever! When groups first form, women may be challenged to ride the surf. As one of my wise friends, Lorene Wapotich, reminded me, groups have dynamics. Through Lorene, I learned a modern truth about the creation of circles that she learned from our friend, Rick Medrick.

Easily, in a short three or four months, new group dynamics can take even the best leaders through honeymoon and best behavior stages that lead to *storming*. Lorene wrote, "Storming is the inevitable stage where conflict erupts in the group, people's buttons get pushed, there is disagreement. This is a pivotal time for the group, how the conflict is handled will determine what happens next." Set aside the egos that produced the conflict and remember the vision of creating for the girls something you didn't receive. There are such rich rewards beyond the storming stage. Women learn from every relationship experience we've ever had. Later our lessons will be reabsorbed by osmosis because they were shared with our daughters and granddaughters. As Jean Shinoda Bolen wrote, "...actually the more you've learned in relationships, the more you have to offer a circle."

Think of the softly falling Spring rains upon the Earth. In her essential feminine nature, Earth calls gentle rains in order to nurture her seeds. So it is with a circle. The essence of a woman's circle will evolve through intention and clarity. Call to you what you most need. To be a significant part of your circle, women must agree to meet regularly and be on time. Everything said in the circle, stays in the circle with the same intention and clarity. There probably will be a check-in so each participant can communicate her level of energy and emotion, each woman shares a bit of her present journey. Each circle group, if organic, will find ways for women to connect at the soul level. To move away from the social chatter that comes with gathering together, you might begin the circle by ringing a bell. A moment of silence following the bell's echo will establish centeredness. Such a ritual will completely shift the energy. The goal is to call forth feminine values of relationship and interdependency to balance our hierarchical culture of dominance through power. The circle will take care of itself because every woman present is both a learner and a teacher. The wisdom of the circle itself calls forth our best qualities and massages them with love and trust, the two greatest gifts girls receive from women.

I recommend a talking piece to facilitate the attention of the group. From Mother Earth, many things may serve as a deserving artwork to pass around the circle, a rock, a root, or a tiny woven vessel. When each person touches such a symbol, their essence blends with the Earth and the object gains a sacred energy. The purpose of a talking piece gives one woman or one girl the floor and she receives deep listening from all the others. With girls, when the piece goes around, often their thoughts become paralyzed in the short twelve inches from their brain to their heart, so nothing comes out of their mouth. Give girls permission to say, "Pass for now," and the sacred object will come back to them. Perhaps it needs to go around three or four times before the paralysis dissolves into a desire to be heard.

We all desire to be heard—that's a woman thing; we all *need* to be heard—that's a human thing. Begin with what is true for you right now. How are you, really? I called an elder circle during the winter months a couple of years ago. The "how are you, really" question kept the circle going week after week. We hardly had time to discuss any of the topics that were written on neatly folded papers in our meeting basket. Encourage young girls to express their emotions, for those feelings are the gauge by which women grow themselves. Each circle called to support girls' life journey will teach her how it feels to be loved and accepted unconditionally. We all need judgment-free environments to find our wings, to twirl and swirl and hear ourselves speak what is locked in our heart-minds.

† † †

In a circle where none of the girls have begun bleeding, they need to discuss their future menses to remove any fear in the group. Welcome the apparition of fear, speak the words that acknowledges her presence, for that is the only way to begin dispelling the energy she holds around this subject. It's an old power that now must die of natural causes. Imagine the transformation when, instead of dreading it, girls want their period each month. It goes on and on with such regularity! If girls wanted and looked forward to their beginning menstrual experience as a glorious first step on their path to womanhood, imagine the shift for all of humanity?

First, girls need to anticipate their very own celebration of bleeding. Each girl carries thousands of maturing eggs from her special ancestral lineage—the blend of her mother's egg, which melted together with her father's sperm. From that auspicious beginning, each girl needs to be aware that another splendid match is carried within each of her eggs, new life possibility exists again and again. For the opportunity to carry new life, a celebration must be organized to honor her special heritage.

All of the details of a ceremony for Puberty Rites must be planned far in advance of the first drops of blood. Set in motion a ritual, perhaps as simple as candle lit seclusion, that can be followed then personalized, embellished, and cherished month after month. Every time a young woman bleeds, the event marks the release of the nutrients that would have carried on her ancestral lineage. Until a young woman desires to claim motherhood, the bleeding each month will be a celebration of her spirit's widest opening. Some women feel their most creative powers during the week of their bleeding, others when the egg drops down the fallopian tube. The awareness of the spiritual veil becoming transparent is one of woman's most sacred experiences and that awareness makes her juices flow easier.

Girls' bodies first signal their own readiness for a passage, then their spirit invites their awareness that a portal doorway is opening. Women's own intuition must be open to the signals, both true and false. Girls' inclination will soon be followed by their inner voices chattering both positive and negative messages. How were we schooled about the voices of confusion, criticism, denial, guilt, or fear? When change looms, our booming inner voices need soothing and quieting. Many girls have had "the talk." Not enough girls are afforded the luxury of spiritual space or time away to be alone with their spirit. Alone time grows into a sacred space that serves a lifetime of inner exploration and personal development. As Shakti Gawain would say, "Stillness can be a very blissful state."

Begin early, long before puberty to allow for girls' softest transitions. I suggest a party atmosphere for the youngest girls between ages seven and ten, because they have left early childhood behind. When girls are first welcomed into the women's circle, it is a very big step for them. Watchful women will know when to begin preparations for Puberty Rites. Look for body hair, breast development and facial features that dissolve her girlish look. The first signs of a girl's development are signals to design and choreograph a future event, but one need not panic over the training bras. A girl's development is gradual enough to make plans and invent challenges. From training bras to menarche is eighteen to forty-eight months. For her first Moon Lodge, each girl who has sat in women's circles can be filled with excited anticipation instead of dread. In women's circles there are hundreds of topics, not just this one. Puberty Rites are a transition for girls, to be sure, but not necessarily the transformative step where they can claim womanhood. Even this, of course, is not cast in stone.

Girls need to be proactively involved in their circle experiences. They will be introduced to ritual and ceremony as a blended gift from the women. Girls who learn to enjoy silence and times when busy-ness just stops will not dominated by doing, maybe even their chattering inner voices will be quieted. Learning to set the stage for luminous moments begins in the company of women. Every facet of girls' development toward wholeness is the reason for calling a circle. An arena that focuses on celebration and change, as in Puberty Rites and Rites of Passage, can be perfectly demonstrated in a community of women who circle because that is what girls need.

When a girl's first Moon-time nears, plans need to be made to create a celebration that marks the most important passage of her youth. This is the one initiation that is common for pre-adults worldwide. A girl's first ceremony marks Puberty Rites, since most girls are too young for womanhood initiations. That is another ritual to plan later. Both boys and girls move into a space where childhood is no longer theirs, yet adulthood is not theirs either. Victor Turner borrowed a descriptive phrase—betwixt and between. Puberty is marked by a universal biological ticker, when the teenage girl is neither an adult nor a child; her time for first menses is very near. In aboriginal cultures, adults separated the pre-pubescent and produced trials and challenges to create a humbling experience. A girl's first days of blood flowing mark the death of one phase of her life which creates a temporary void and gives birth to the next. Many of our life's changes follow the same urgency as winter giving way to spring—an urgency we can understand. A native vision quest is one way to dramatize or emphasize the transition or experience. The late Steven Foster's experiences and wisdom are found in *The Book of the Vision Quest*, where he provides answers to innumerable questions about what is involved in a modern day vision quest. Many teen age girls do quest for a vision that somewhat coincides with their maturity.

Girls approach the threshold of their transformation with no thought of change, yet with all her thoughts on the conditions that will make her a woman. What she does not know is that the biological-physical, social, emotional and spiritual elements converge in the portal that she enters when her monthly menstrual cycle signals that her change time has arrived. Hopefully, before the actual menses begins, this girl has finished her personal bundle of trials and challenges, so she has made herself ready to descend into a sacred place for change. Lucky is the girl who has been prepared to activate carefully laid plans.

What follows are just my thoughts, I don't know the creative level of your circle and I don't know the prepubescent girl who is ready for her Puberty Rites. At the very liminal moment, maybe she will be secreted away for a few days of privacy, maybe she will lay low in her room or maybe she will take the guest room while her room is being redone. Perhaps she will be transported to a cave or a mountain-top to be alone. Know that she is in a transition space where nothing feels familiar. The portal of transformation comes from an altered state of consciousness. While things seem like a dark and swirling vortex of energy, much is happening in the subconscious and in the spirit. She needs deep silence for her confused state. There is work being done on the spiritual level like an unraveling. She needs waited on and pampered. After three, four, or five days of being sequestered in some way, she needs her circle of women friends to surround her, to celebrate her, to allow all the changes that ran through her mind to settle back into the ordinary. She needs to speak with the voice of a woman, for that is the cause for celebration. By listening, celebrating, feasting and dancing, her circle will assist with something known as reincorporation, when life can return to the mundane.

If women around the circle will create a careful plan and timeline for each pre-pubescent girl, the Puberty Rites will become a cornerstone for womanhood. Girls will know the meaning of sacred and will never again confuse it with mundane. Each girl will know her own ritual and will spend time each month connecting to her Divine Feminine nature. Truly becoming an active participant in her circle, each girl, one by one, will share and volunteer as a woman, and will anticipate her next step, her Rites of Passage ceremony.

Graphic discussions about the sexual act may be postponed until mothers agree the time is right. As some point, perhaps shortly after a girl's Puberty Rites, as each girl joins the ranks of women, she needs an open discussion about sex. Adolescents today are franker about their sexuality than any previous generation. Sensuous and sexual are ambitious goals for girls who have no experience. Mother, consider yourself the last one she will talk to about the sexual act, unless you choose to be the first one. I recommend lifting the lid on this taboo and using all the time before she leaves home, between a girl's puberty ceremony and her womanhood ceremony, as a time when women speak frankly. For each young woman, there will be thousands of questions and connection threads around sexuality and sensuality, she needs to get answers from someone. Actually, she may seem to be an endless stream of questions, so if you create the stage for questioning, it will increase her comfort level. Perhaps the girls in the circle will have a questioning time before the end of each gathering. A little reading by everyone on the subjects of body image, sensuality, masturbation, sex toys will make for lively circle discussions if you all dare. Naomi Wolff's *Promiscuities* is her biographical accounting of the days when free sex was in vogue. It is still relevant to where girls are headed when they leave the protection of their parents' nest. The book, *The Body Project* by Joan Jacobs Brumberg, is fascinating reading for a history of women's body image. However, the pop culture has a leading edge that is difficult to stay current with, so I recommend the girls be invited to lead this discussion. Women's circles are the perfect arena to create a level of trust and comfort where women and girls can have open conversations about everything.

Without planning everything very far in advance, women's circles continue for years with no risk of running out of subjects. Think collectively about your lives, and ask what topics interest your group. You might start with gardening, nutrition and cooking, cleaning and fung shui-ing your home spaces. Then there's beauty, makeup, dress, thriving, differences and similarities of dualities, intuition, sensory perception, balance, harmony, peace, relationships, dominated or partnership kinds of relationships, mothers, grandmothers, men, archetypes, charkas, energy—each one of the circles could have a theme. Hopefully, circles grow into earth-based skills as challenges for girls between monthly meetings. Then, there will be all the kingdoms of Nature to talk about. The agenda need not be filled in when the circle opens. Mothers will invite the girls to share and in the sharing women will learn to listen to girls. Plan activities for only half your time, the girls and nature will take care of the other half.

The biggest malady in adolescence today is that the girls are not listened to well enough, causing their voices to sink down into their spirits. Watching their mothers, grandmothers and other teachers, girls are not even certain they agree with the modern concept of womanhood. In their fantasy minds, girls can and do create utopias where life resembles cherry blossoms—pink, soft and quite perfect. The circle is a quiet safe place to share dreams of utopias. From those visions, girls can create intentions that are real and powerful. Women know the paradox of being like our mothers while we try so hard to be different. A double whammy happens to girls around age eleven or twelve, when they are confronted with patriarchy. It's never a pretty event when girls become aware that we live in a "man's world."

Without womanhood training, when adolescence happens to girls, they feel like they are dragged along by a runaway train. Women and girls who sit in circle have a sanctuary to offer each other. One day, patriarchy will lose its power, though that has not happened in my life time. Women are still dominated in families by their fathers and husbands. We are certainly dominated by mega-corporations and the men who run them. To date the leadership in this country is dominated by men. Around the world, women in other countries have vastly different experiences and their degrees of domination cover a wide spectrum. Women can strive for, even insist on, a spiritual partnership in all our relationships, but we will only know of that possibility if we have some training in womanhood. Otherwise, girls will not even know enough about relationships or partnerships to make an informed choice. Without choice or awareness, as we know, the school of hard knocks is ready to teach us about patriarchy and domination. Circles are beautiful arenas for conscious choice training for individuation and development.

⚤ ⚤ ⚤

When women move away from their mothers for the first time, a new kind of freedom emerges. At age seventeen or eighteen they are still women-becoming. However, they will feel a sense of freedom for discovery of self and true independence. Mothers can hope for a consequence from all the years of nurturing and protection, young women will also need interdependence. When they leave home, we still want our girls to need us. A part of us never lets go, and that is the interdependence part. We need each other, our joy quotient needs to be needed even when we are apart. That need is for connection, for the mutual counselors that we have become for each other. As she individuates from her mother, each woman devises her own way and a life for herself. There is strength and beauty in that, but go back through the days when there was struggle and anguish there, too. Girls need to become independent to experience the freedom of their own souls. After that, they need to weave their way back into their home community or into a new community they call home.

Especially if girls have grown up in women's circles, they will be emotionally connected to community. When they re-create community for themselves, they will draw from rich experience and know how to create a social family with women in the new place they call home. This is what circles demonstrate for girls through all their years of becoming a woman. The joyous truth is mothers and daughters need each other in womanhood, we need to integrate strength, love, trust, courage and harmony with our need for each other. With a strong weave, we will always feel the family connection. To remain close and connected, we must learn and practice forgiveness. All the decades of the 20th Century are filled with stories of disharmony between mothers and daughters. Now is the time, through women and girls' council circles, to create a New Story for our lives and for our relationships.

Finally, girls need women who are willing to grow with them and create ritual, ceremony and celebrations. Developmental changes are both subtle and dramatic. Celebrations, however, are psychological, women need them too. Passages do not end in adolescence. Think of changes as passages, a word that the writer Gail Sheehy made famous. Passages or portals for transformation are all of one weave. There are portals for love, marriage, births, for losses and for relocations. There are so many change agents in a woman's life, unnoticed, they can damage one's psychic wellbeing. A portal opens when a woman's genes signal the beginning of a developmental change, a psychological change or an environmental change, a portal opens. She can move through gracefully, intentionally, and with personal power, or she can resist. Resistance for any reason will cause damage and some wounding. Resistance takes you out of flow. A portal refused, denied, or unacknowledged causes a small hole in one's psychic fabric. Such holes need to be mended, sooner or later. Many women go to their graves with holes, real-life wounds that are not articulated. Those old women feel sadness, regret, and even bitterness. They aren't even sure why, because too much life has happened. Think of psychic holes as grief, remorse and resentment. These cold, hard, negative emotions are all preventable.

Look deep inside your heart, this women's work is also about healing and answering the question, "What do I wish I had when I was eight or twelve or sixteen?" This work is passed down from ancient women, our ancestors. Those grandmothers knew about belonging, they knew how to cure a longing, how to weave a net of safety around emotions, around the psychic, around the physical well-being of young girls. For the simple question, "What do I wish I had?" my list of answers is long. I would wish for a better relationship with my mother, a clearer understanding about womanhood, a thorough discussion of choices and better knowledge about how the world would knock me around. I wish I had interconnectedness and interdependence. I wish I had some clue about balance and wholeness. As a young woman, I didn't even know those words.

Look at the Risk List in Appendix B in the back. When you remember yourself at age twelve or sixteen, what shows up first? This may take some truth telling in a journal session. Then look at this list for your daughter, coming up a generation after you. Many risks arise because parents are in denial, sad to say. If we can be honest about this list of risks, we can help girls. Each of the risks I succumbed to left a psychic hole that I've had to heal.

♦ ♦ ♦

One of the hallmarks of femininity is silence. Women need to teach girls about sitting in silence. When the time is right, one of the circle members should introduce nature meditation, which involves sitting in silence. Finding the gaps in one's thoughts creates the opening for a girl to become part of the natural world. Being in sacred space with a fire-light, even with a small candle, is women's most ancient way of being, it's the feminine difference. Girls need to learn to sit in silence with nature to sort through all their chattering messages. Women can make a ceremony out of everything—morning, appreciation, inner guidance, journal writing, purification, women's circle of support, bedtime, a new year, a new home, birthdays, retirement, elder-hood, welcoming the unknown, balancing, weddings, clearing out the past, releasing an old relationship, divorce, conscious holidays, death—in between all these events, we will hold all of life together much easier if we can make time to just *be*.

My friend, Kathleen, who is introduced in the next chapter, embodies ceremony. She teaches the four parts of a ceremony are setting intention, asking for protection, grounding your energy, and finally releasing through surrender. Sitting in silence with a question is a ceremony, so is journaling, painting, and making dinner. Ceremony and playfulness are so closely related, they are delightfully intertwined. Set an intention, tend to protection and grounding and share ceremony with the girls you love. It will seem like magic, but they will grow into incredible, reverent, and mature women. Girls need women who are willing to share their entire selves. Girls simply need time with women. Between the years from eight to eighteen, girls need more women, more often, in fact, the more women the better. An idea for community building is adopt a sister circle. Twice a year, maybe on the Equinox months, exchange pot luck lunches. Call a Solstice celebration for all the circles in the county, the valley, or the city. These are just creative thoughts leaking out.

Although each of us can only share so much and listen so much, when girls are offered many strong role models, womanhood's secret magical formula for thriving will emerge. As we nurture, protect and care for our girls, they themselves will extract our wisdom. They will locate things inside of us we don't even know were concealed. They will pull until we are all richer, wiser and happier, until we release all our secrets for thriving. As the seasons roll into years, your circle will know how to thrive because of the connectedness that is created by women. This is the biggest secret of all. Our magic formula for thriving has no value to anyone else unless we are willing to give it away. By merely spending time, our magic secrets become someone else's nugget of gold. All those delicious tidbits of wisdom are not on the surface nor should they be shared all at once. My recommendation is that you find a special way to come together as a group in order to discover women's wisdom together. Experience is everything. Women have it, girls want it. Talking and sharing will prevent girls' experiences from going into dangerous territory.

As a backdrop for circles, Earth-based adventures will offer challenges and delights for girls eight to eighteen. Nature is my recommended risk preventor. Girls need to become intimate with nature in order to become fully mature. You might think this is a bold statement, but nature will teach girls to be contemplative, thoughtful, generous, hopeful, protective, still and whole. These qualities and more come to a person who spends at least one quiet hour every day, observing everything in nature. All of the situations that people label problems can be unraveled in the stillness of nature.

Sitting in silence is expansive and experiential and so is movement. That's literally anything that involves getting the whole body out of a chair and engaged. One of the strongest experiences for children comes through movement, whether it's moving through the woods, moving on bicycles, moving with others, moving to music or moving to drum beats—particularly drumming while they chant something. When girls use their bodies, their brains engage in building scaffolding that will connect to all their academic subjects, for they are literally making space in the mind for information to be stored.

Nature offers serendipity, an expanding level of awareness that is co-creative. Psychologists call this processing and identify it as a behavior that is centuries older than psychology! Our planet desperately needs a fully aware generation, for they have inherited a bundle of challenges. Nature defines us with more clarity and precision than any other relational connection we have. Time spent in nature begins with mind chatter and eventually unfolds into an illumined and accurate definition of our inner selves. This is also known as dirt time and it promises to make us brilliant.

Later on, I prescribe naturalist mentoring and play for girls who are developing into women. The next chapter offers inspiration and encouragement for mothers of girls who need and want to create a Rites of Passage ceremony. A girl's glorious path to womanhood depends on acknowledging her movement, she needs to know when she has arrived.

4

Rites of Passage into Womanhood

An Indian Prayer

*O GREAT SPIRIT, Whose voice I hear in the winds, and whose
breath gives life to all the world,*

Hear me! I am small and weak, I need your strength and wisdom.

*LET ME WALK IN BEAUTY, and make my eyes ever behold
the red and purple sunset.*

MAKE MY HANDS *respect the things you have made and my
ears sharp to hear your voice.*

*MAKE ME WISE so that I may understand the things you have
taught my people.*

*LET ME LEARN the lessons you have hidden in every leaf and
rock.*

*I SEEK STRENGTH, not to be greater than my brother or
sister, but to fight my greatest enemy—myself.*

*MAKE ME ALWAYS READY to come to you with clean hands
and straight eyes.*

*SO WHEN LIFE FADES, as the fading sunset, my spirit may
come to you without shame.*

—Offered by the Sioux Indian Children
Of the Red Cloud Indian School
Pine Ridge, South Dakota

Long ago, in all the corners of the world, Rites of Passage or ritual initiation ceremonies for spiritual transformations designated and honored each change from cradle to grave. Very little of how ritual initiations were practiced was passed down, very little survived the obliteration of the past several centuries. Traditions long lost from most of our world cultures cannot easily be recreated. Women have no connecting experience, so most of us don't know what to do or when. There's some fear in that unknown. We fear doing the wrong thing, so we hesitate to do anything.

I want to dispel that fear by filling in a few blanks. There is a fair amount to learn about ritual initiations, mostly from anthropologists and also from Elders who refused to let their traditions die. In the following story you will see that I was propelled by the same wisdom I want to pass along to you—Just do it! With the support of your women's circle, make the preparations and do the ceremonies! Follow the formula if you like, be as creative as your muse inspires, but without a ritual initiation, the girl's wound is deep. Just do it! In my first leap of faith doing a Rites of Passage ceremony, the courage required was negligible compared to the greatness of her experience.

Victor Turner is the anthropologist who first wrote of the psychological benefits of Rites of Passage, although Arnold van Gennep is the one who coined the term. In 1974, Turner wrote, "Ritual is a principal means by which society grows and moves into the future."

Rituals rise from the collective hearts of a women's community. Rituals for girls' passages must be considered and prepared far in advance of the event. Although, like a wedding, they can be made elaborate or complex, initiations or Rites of Passages are not necessarily difficult, they can be wonderfully simple. Just like, from Idaho, I wouldn't tell you how to do your daughter's wedding in Vermont, I will only give you the necessary steps for an initiation ceremony. Most of the fun is how you and the elders in your community fill in the details.

It's the girl who must be prepared. While Puberty Rites are signaled by biological changes that take over two years to complete, transitions yet to come for womanhood's fullest bloom are also cognitive, social and emotional. A girl must find reception in her peer group before, during and after the event. She wants and needs to be recognized as a woman by all her family and friends. She wants assurances that she has journeyed somewhere and arrived. The energy of the portal is lost if she feigns great resistance or discounts the ritual all together.

In 1969, Turner wrote of the change agent that I have called the portal of confusion, "Liminality is a state of being in between phases. In a rite of passage the individual in the liminal phase is neither a member of the group she previously belonged to nor is she a member of the group she will belong to upon the completion of the rite. The most obvious example is the teenager who is neither an adult nor a child. Liminal entities are neither here nor there; they are betwixt and between."

Rites of Passage or Womanhood Initiations are age appropriate, each girl must be *called* to claim her womanhood. Adult responsibilities carry such a weight that each young woman-becoming must be certain she is ready to carry the added stress and power of womanhood. With younger siblings, girls often assume grown-up responsibilities as a pre-teenager, so they seem mature at thirteen or fourteen. Other circumstances cause an early ripening, certain losses or death of a parent, for instance. Anytime after age sixteen, women and girls of the circle can expect the *call to womanhood* will come to the girl or her mother, hopefully both simultaneously. Appearance, demeanor, accountability, community service, caring for children and elders, superior performance on skills and challenges are all signs of her *call to womanhood*. Women and elders of the circle will confer about the proof or readiness of womanhood, then question the girl, then instigate the plans that have long been prepared for her.

Those preparations are a choreography created by the women in the circle, a girl's mother, her elders and the woman-becoming. Probably the only part the girl will know about is the opening and closing ritual which the woman-becoming can design with the help of certain women

in the circle. Perhaps she will get help with a beautiful written pro-
nouncement, a poem, or a thanksgiving address. An essential part of the
preparations are the challenges that both stretch and reward the
woman-becoming, she must be tested. With a combination of skills
demonstrated, leadership challenges, community service, and creative
expression, women can easily put each girl through a test for womanhood that she will love and remember. Each girl's choreography will be
unique, but so well planned that once the *call to womanhood* is agreed
upon, a month or two or three may be required for the fulfillment.
Excitement builds as the woman-becoming accepts her challenges from
women watching, it's all part of the fun. Almost anything can be
included but, like her puberty ritual, mind, body and spirit need to be
engaged. From shopping trips to lengthy solo times, the impact for each
girl will be different. What will engage her, test her, complete her, and
thrill her? Those are the surprises that women should include in the
choreography for Womanhood Initiations.

The initiation *formula*, as it's been preserved, has always had three
steps and as many details within each to delight both the women and
the girls holding the circle. The first step is *severance*. In this step all the
preparations must be made before the girl actually severs from her parents. The second step called the *threshold* or portal is prepared by other
women of her circle and her Elders. Once the *threshold* is crossed, that
is, once a girl moves into the portal, she is in an in-between world, a
place known as betwixt and between. This is an obvious place for a
Death Lodge or a ritual that symbolizes the end of childhood or youth.
For instance, a specific symbol may be created to symbolize her girlhood, and at somewhere in the choreography, the symbol is ritually
buried or burned to demonstrate change. From a death-of-girlhood
ceremony, a rebirth is a natural occurrence and the void begins something new. For step one, *severance*, and step two, crossing the *threshold*
into the portal, you need to plan actions that are meaningful for the initiate. Don't rush, perhaps events can spread out for a week or even a
fortnight. The middle step, in the portal between adolescence and
adulthood, is where a journey of trials can be contained, prolonged just

long enough to allow for completion of the tests. Please include ample reflection time. The third and final step—*reincorporation*—is ritually marked by stepping over the threshold again, when the initiate returns as an adult and normalcy resumes. Change occurs during this three-step process. The skin of adolescence is shed and is replaced by a cloak of adulthood, *reincorporation* will be equally invisible. Transformation occurs within the movement from a normal state to an altered state of consciousness then back to a new normal, a new psychological state. Mother and Grandmother are important players immediately following the young woman's re-entry. After she crosses back over her threshold, all of her reincorporation activities are meant to flood a newly blossomed woman in the magnificent and glorious light of womanhood. For the woman-becoming, completion of these steps will feel like a peak experience, and part of her new responsibility will be to make the change visible. Actions speak louder than words.

Around this formula, which has survived the centuries of near-dormancy, women from the circle are at liberty to demonstrate their best rituals. Certainly, the completion of this passage of transformation necessitates a ceremony to bring the newly initiated woman back into her circle with a celebratory community gathering. Include dressing beautifully, perhaps like Goddesses, incorporate flowers, candles, and music, surely. Contemplate how to summon the wider community to present her first steps of womanhood through opening, presentation, and closing ceremonies followed by speeches, gifting, and feasting. Women have genes that remember how to make a wonderful and lasting impact on the new woman. Women—don't hesitate, don't be shy, this culmination is one of those days to be remembered forever. Finally, the new woman can express her emotions and gratitude and even commit to her first actions as an adult. Elders will find a way to hold her accountable, then everyone returns to their new normal together.

To enter our initiate's passage in the story that follows, my co-creators and I used the *formula* that began with our acknowledgment of the woman-becoming. Her *readiness* and *separation* combined for stage one. After she was *separated* from her mother, that detachment was made more poignant in the wilderness. As you will see, we lingered in the margin or *limin* (in Latin it means threshold) of stage two to increase her comfort, to add drama and amplify her anticipation. While we were at the *threshold* in stage two, inside the passage portal, we worked five days to prepare our initiate for stage three. After a marathon session to clearly define womanhood, she was trained in the art of questioning other women. We spent one full day pulling her through trials in her portal toward stage three, her *reincorporation*. At the finale, our new woman knew from experience that her expression of womanhood must come through her voice. Since then, I have conducted other initiations—even telephone consultations. I've learned that the contents of the initiation must fit the occasion. Wrapped up in the bundle that women create together, we must take the best wisdom from the old ways. For womanhood's New Story we must now give birth to simple traditions that can and will be passed from generation to generation. We are dancing and singing to coax this Rites of Passage up and out of the ashes of time. For the women-becoming who pirouette within our circles, the most important part is our action—make the plans and follow through.

Our culture greatly needs elders who have themselves been initiated to perform initiation rites. If you've done your own healing work, you will have remembered your previous liminal phases that were left unattended. Those spirit holes can now be mended. A ritual can and should be performed to acknowledge all the passages or stages that were not ritually acknowledged and celebrated. For women, your list may be long. Your own puberty and womanhood ceremonies were probably passed over, not to mention new jobs, promotions, social memberships and new geographies after marriage. Women who take the time to mourn and heal any uncelebrated transformations will be better prepared for the girls who are women-becoming. Your women's circle offers a forum and a motivation for this healing. Our other stages have often been well celebrated—birthdays, weddings and even births are rituals still common in our culture because of our love for fun and serendipity.

I have a caveat to emphasize the "differences" between our times, now, and the times when initiations were customary. In all cultures worldwide before the 20th Century, Rites of Passage or Initiation or Coming-of-Age rituals were performed only once for girls becoming women. Those old ways are difficult to duplicate because girls experience menarche, their first Moon-time cycles, five years earlier than just a hundred years ago! Simultaneous to this progressively earlier menstrual flow, our culture created a chasm between girlhood and womanhood, the time known as adolescence. As I mentioned earlier, many things contribute to the early onset of girls' menstrual cycles. Perhaps the most prevalent two are an uninterrupted food supply with no cycles of feast and famine, and hormones that are ingested by our animal protein. Until about a hundred years ago, Moon cycles appeared when girls were fifteen to seventeen. Call those the olden days. In their middle to late teen years, young women were more than ready to accept womanhood—spiritually, physically and responsibly. Girlhood gave way to womanhood with no lapse of time like we have now. In the late 1800s, adolescence was culturally created to coincide with mandatory schooling.

Women need to be clear about how mature our girls' are at age twelve and the enormous developmental chasm between ages twelve and sixteen. Women also need to consider the meaning behind ritual initiations. These are wholly new times. We do need a New Story for womanhood. As you read on, you will understand that the fairest young maiden helped me define my own feelings about initiations. Rights and obligations of womanhood are defined differently for girls age twelve verses girls age sixteen. Their adult brains develop around age fourteen, so they comprehend at entirely different levels. Are girls ready for womanhood when their Moon-time begins at eleven or twelve? I believe our girls should receive Puberty Rites for their first Moon-time, followed by years of womanhood trainings inside their women's circle and, finally, a womanhood initiation, a Rites of Passage ceremony and celebration.

For the women who commit to their girls' complete womanhood development, perhaps two celebrations will occur where only one did before. As you will see in Lauren's story, the initiation must fit the girl and her circumstances. Notice how much we learned from Lauren, a wise young maiden who opened our eyes. Girls may be co-creators of *some* of their plans, but most of the details need to be hushed, held secretly, and later unfolded by the women who hold the circle. Women can raise their awareness to detect the warning signals, the psychic alarms. The biological imperative will take girls to the Puberty Rites *threshold* when their bleeding starts. That suggests a time of *separation* and deep introspection, perhaps three days and three nights to be left alone, but attended. In her alone time, a girl's spiritual perception will change her whole worldview. Rather quickly, that time away in silence or perhaps swaying to soft music will become her new normal.

Following Puberty Rites, everything else that makes a woman a woman remains a mystery. Girls need training from women who have found the secrets to thriving. Girls also need skills to build a foundation for confidence and self-esteem. We all know that girls need consistent, confidential and intimate support from a wide group of women, how their needs get filled is the New Story we are co-creating. Girls need both play and spiritual development, they need both nature and men-toring. Women who are creative together can easily sponsor a training for the archetypes that supports all the skills building a girl needs between ages twelve and eighteen (see the book's final page for infor-mation). Think prevention, please. The years between Puberty Rites and Rites of Passage or womanhood initiations are utterly crucial for women-becoming.

A final *threshold* looms. The "empty nest" separation for mother/daughter pairs happens when the younger woman claims her independence. A tight circle of women will know when to initiate each girl. Please remember, initiations must be done one girl at a time because of each girl's unique development path. I encourage women to experiment with ceremony, month after month. Have fun by stretching to elaborate as well as shrinking to simplify, thereby discovering which rituals every-one loves. Play with the classic elements, candles, flowers, drums, and bells. Add recorded music, food, gifting, poetry, arts and crafts. By the time initiates are ready, women's intuition will be the best guide.

I invite you to spend some time contemplating how sacred our mission is to reinstate womanhood initiations. When celebrations were not held for us in the older generations, we knew not how to fill our longing. Some of us felt like we were thrown to the wolves, a wonderful metaphor for the elation of sexual experimentation, but how would our lives have been different if a circle of women offered such trust and intimacy we felt comfortable to search out our answers through questioning rather than through experimentation? In middle to late adolescence, there is such a sexual fire inside, each daughter deserves to have her fire lit by her mother's wisdom and blessings. Before that first special young man enters the picture, stories like *Skeleton Woman* by Clarissa Pinkola Estés must be shared. As we put our creative best toward this New Story for Womanhood, focus on what you wish you had received for your womanhood training, that is exactly what the girls need most on their path to womanhood.

The following is a story of a Rites of Passage and Womanhood Ceremony called *Lauren's Bloom*. Our hope is this story will fire your imagination. Although it could not possibly be copied, all the parts may be borrowed.

Womanhood is a badge of honor for young adolescent women, that honor includes the integration of independence and interdependence, power and empowerment, responsibility and accountability, love and lust, employment and right livelihoods. Our culture is so complex now, that adult identities should not be linked to age or marriage or babies. The inner spirits of girls, like boys, have a window of opportunity that opens when it is time to explore the mysteries. We offered one girl a spiritual training to give her courage to face her unknown potential in search of her deeper selfhood.

From the West Woods, deep inside my heart pocket, I call forth a true story to share with you. Within the folds of this story lay the very foundation of womanhood. A young girl went into the woods to spend a week with three crone women she barely knew. We spiraled down into memories buried deep in our own adolescence in search of the rare, wild orchid known as our bloom. None of us had been offered a Rites of Passage ceremony to usher us into womanhood, so our search took us around the world and back into ancient times. In this soulful search, we discovered the many wounds that had been lodged in our own tender years—cultural, personal, familial, gender and peer wounds. We all store them and our souls remind us of them. Womanhood herself has become wounded, so we searched for a great healing of the collective wounds. Even though cultures vary, girls enter womanhood biologically the same all over the world. In our search, we located multicultural, ancient, indigenous instructions, as well as anthropological research. We are grateful for the many sources that helped us discover the roots of womanhood. This true story is our give-away.

Across the abyss of all human time, womanhood celebrations have been gifted from elder women who assessed maidens for physical indicators, responsible attitudes, increased accountability and their heart-soul requests. This journey to meet the heroine within beckons early in life and pesters and festers deep down if it's ignored. We gifted an initiation experience because Lauren was poised on the edge of her glorious bloom and her mother heard her answer the call to womanhood.

Just before Lauren's Rites of Passage began, I whispered the introductory prayer for thanksgiving. In reverence, natural things appear crisp. Dappled sunbeams reached the forest floor. In this soft corner of the Planet Earth, deep in the Rockies, grasses were tall, the flowers taller. When Diana, Kathleen and I offered this journey, we entered our true self-archetypes—I as the Visionary, Kathleen as the Teacher, and Diana as the Healer. Kathleen lives this story. A little pixie, with a bright fairie face, Kathleen knows Passages like the Ancient Ones did. Coming from faraway, Diana is completely devoted to growth and dearly loves a good adventure. Thrilled for the company of my dear friends, I was humbly honored to have their help. We hugged, cried, shared a meal and a tent. As our joyful tears washed away the years apart, our souls created a new strand on the web that binds us together—we celebrate women and all our passages.

Nearly thirteen, eldest daughter in a family of four children, Lauren was a fair, shy and willowy girl who came to the wild woods of Idaho to learn about womanhood. Lauren's mother, Geri, brought the spiritual power of a woman in her extraordinary bloom. We received her sincere gratitude. With no hesitation about her role, Geri modeled a life loved and lived well. Lauren and Geri arrived ready for all of our surprises. In full summer, the light on the high peaks created drama from sunrise to sunset. We were lucky to borrow Kathleen's beautiful vision quest camp and her council tipi for Lauren's Rite of Passage.

Respectfully and ceremonially, as taught by our indigenous friends, we gathered in front of the tipi and smudged each other with sage to open our senses and dissipate lingering nervousness. Besides smudging because it's a nice ritual, the smoke of sage neutralizes negative energy. Our teachers have always dedicated an offering of thanks to "all our relations." Softly, I say prayers whenever I smudge someone. "Feel your connection to our Ancestors. Give thanks to the Great Spirit for all our blessings." Through the soles of our feet, we pull up Earth's energies, which transform all of our resistant vibrations.

After offering gratitude to Mother Earth, we entered the tipi and walked sun-wise to begin with grace and peace. I introduced the talking stick, another custom symbolically used in circles for respect. I gave thanks to all our hosts in the natural world and for women's passages. Passage seems such an ordinary word for pivotal moments that contain the essential mysteries of life.

Lauren answered the call to separate from her mother and go on an guided adventure into womanhood. After five days of trials and skills building, she would descend alone into silent space where soul meets body and mind. If she emerged as a woman from her cocoon-space, a celebration would follow. That was the challenge Lauren accepted when she chose this journey. Her experience would be slowly integrated over time through her inner dialogue.

After our ceremonial opening, we needed a camp orientation. With a walk about, we filled women's natural need to belong to our place. We noted how the mountains cradled our encampment and observed the thousands of sego lilies that bobbed their heads in greetings. Each one of us blended energies with the ancient ones who passed down women's wisdom. As Nature opened our awareness, we were rewarded with lots of animal tracks, hawks, butterflies, elephant head flowers, wolf spiders, yellow monkey flowers and dense evergreen forests. Women, who hold space for the growth potential of each other, provide loving energy for the growth of all of humankind. When Lauren's heroine journey began, she entered the mystique where her quest would be slowly revealed.

We marked our threshold with flags as a portal for those undertaking a journey and sent mother and daughter off through the journey's portal. Lauren and Geri used songlines to go into the wilderness and back. Mother to daughter, and daughter to mother, they would share "remember when" stories. With no mention of her subconscious, Lauren entered an altered state of being when she stepped over her threshold. She went betwixt and between into the portal of confusion.

After several long hours, Kathleen, Diana and I stood at the threshold and beat our drums. They returned mute. I received looks from Geri and Lauren that told me they had just had a really good time together. Their blended look of love and peace was heartwarming because they had shared precious memories. The whole world might be healed with such feelings.

In silence, Diana directed them into the tipi for a creative time of journal-writing. For countless souls, ourselves included, journal-writing heals perceptions and emotions, as it records celebrations that come and go. Years go by and journals create order out of the wonderful, the awful and the ordinary events that flow through our lives. Diana invited Geri and Lauren to symbolize openness and freedom by imagining an intention statement that would guide their future relationship. On their own talking stick, a secret intention was written down and buried beneath a ribbon. A long pause in the drama of this first day occurred while they wrote in their journals and decorated their talking stick.

† † †

Before dawn I awakened to a light heart. Something magical had happened in my dreamtime—anxiety and self-judgment were transformed. When the veil of night lifted, another sky-blue Idaho day was revealed. The birds were raucous and I felt so steeped in joy, I barely noticed the ice on my shoelaces. Within the cellular level of my instincts, ancestors blazed the trail and left marks on my soul. Early that first morning with mother and daughter sleeping in camp with us, I realized this was both the past and the future for women. As I sauntered around the camp perimeter, the ambient light on the mountain peaks reminded me of wildness and of Thoreau's words, "In wildness is the preservation of the world." On that morning when Geri and Lauren trusted their journey to our holy intentions, we would call forth wildness for the preservation of womanhood.

When we gathered and moved carefully around the kitchen tent, our breakfast bonding began. True to who we are, the spirit of play rose up through our feet and tickled our tummies from the inside as we bumped butts by the stove. Kathleen's tent kitchen was just one body wide, so we circled the center aisle and laughed as we squeezed around each other. Spiritually, joy is the only attitude we need to lead with if we want others to follow.

In the heroine's journey myth, bonding and separation symbolically occupy the beginning. To enlarge and transform their kinship, Geri and Lauren stepped beyond their mother and daughter relationship. During Lauren's pilgrimage to womanhood, they would separate so they could reunite as women together in the world. On the edge of her bloom, Lauren sat in the tipi with a hot chocolate beside her and her favorite stuffed animal to cuddle for strength. She looked up through her lashes into each woman's face and sensed the allure of womanhood. Each of us checked in as the talking stick was passed. We spoke of sleep and dreams to clear fears and doubts. One by one, we settled into a risk-taking place, where our spirits wanted to stretch out of our comfort zones. To demonstrate risk, I asked each woman to tell a mother/daughter story from her childhood memories. Geri and Lauren both hesitated, since their freshly stirred memories were sacred, private moments. New relationship ties began because we laughed and cried together when our ears were blessed with poignant and happy personal memories. Our words belonged to the circle and naturally remained in its center when we left.

Next, we learned about life stages based on ancient Medicine Wheel teachings offered by Kathleen. After a brief introduction of the symbolism of the cardinal directions, we transformed an open meadow into a Wheel. Like little ants, we busily gathered long sticks to outline the Wheel's design and marked out four quadrants on the inside. The Medicine Wheel became our prayer space, an arena for spiritual teachings, and our ceremonial stage. From our efforts to build and design the Wheel, our camaraderie shifted. Glowing, we settled into camp chairs to learn more about the symbolic language of the Medicine Wheel and how it influences our well-being.

For our imaginations, Kathleen painted images with the Medicine Wheel. As symbols, the four directions represent the birth, bloom, death and rebirth in Nature. In parallel, these same directions represent the four ages of humans—child, adolescent, adult and elder. Having been taught by indigenous elders, Kathleen passes their teachings down and around. Psychologically and emotionally, our minds play a big role in how we view our lives.

With her blessings and offerings, Kathleen prepared the Wheel as a stage. For most mothers and daughters, their relationship stretches and changes from their very first separation through many, many others. Ritual separations encourage everyone to accept a young girl into womanhood because our genetic expectations understand initiations are spiritually and psychologically important. For Geri and Lauren, we provided a symbolic umbilical cord of beautiful ½-inch hemp tied with purple on the ends. When mother and daughter faced each other,

Kathleen wrapped the cord around them in an infinity symbol, a figure eight. She blended her words of wisdom with Judith Duerk's profound inquiry from *Circle of Stones*:

> How might your life have been different if there had been a place for you, a place for you to go to be with your mother, with your sisters and the aunts, with your grandmothers, and the great- and great-great-grandmothers, a place of women to go, to be, to return to, as women? How might your life be different?

From the heart of their connection, Geri spoke her truth to Lauren about what this separation meant, what love means and what their future might hold. She placed a little gift in Lauren's palm to empower her journey. Through her tears, Lauren accepted her gift and echoed a similar message to Geri. Knowing theirs would be a long relationship, Kathleen handed the scissors to daughter and mother to cut their cord in half. With no further words, Geri took her half of the symbolic umbilical cord and departed. Since Geri and Lauren felt enough trust to separate, when they next looked into each other's eyes, Lauren would be a fully initiated woman, transformed by ancient wisdom.

We hope that the experiences of love and trust, of play and joy, of reverence and wholeness, will reach around the globe and enter into the hearts of every human being. Since this celebratory book for girls' path to womanhood is offered to those who would lend a hand to girls along their journey, these suggestions are written as a restorative for all women.

Not too far away, a small, nearly-dry creek was flowing. We used this opportunity to enter Nature as women's way to reintegrate our energies. Like children, we walked down into the creek bed, we were curious about every little thing. In a playful way we re-created a bonding as old as all the time humans have walked the earth. Kathleen challenged us to find heart rocks. We looked and looked and found water bugs, spider webs, mysterious plants, and a couple of good heart-shaped rocks.

Overtaken by the wonders of the natural world, we were transported back in time. We stepped into the lives of our ancestors.

Lauren skipped and danced around in the passage-way between her childhood and her womanhood—she was betwixt and between. Around the fire that night, we sensed her hesitancy to join our conversations. We kept it light and funny before going to bed early. Lauren moved her tent to be near ours and then moved her sleeping bag into my tent for a closeness that made us both smile into our dreamtime.

♀   ♀   ♀

As the second day dawned, Diana, Kathleen and I held council by the fire and watched the early morning sun bring warmth to the world. I talked with my friends about a study by Lyn Brown and Carol Gilligan, two Harvard researchers who uncovered the early adolescent tendency for girls to hide their voices deep inside for safety. At this stage in Lauren's developmental journey, her hesitancy was more than a trust issue. We needed to encourage Lauren to find and use her voice. All of the expressions about her emergence into womanhood would determine how her woman-spirit would blossom.

We took lawn chairs, lunch and three dogs, and piled into Kathleen's truck for play and sunshine at the lake. Lauren was the first one in the lake and, just like a water baby, coaxed all of us in. Kathleen dived in, Diana went bravely step-by-step, and then Lauren came out and pushed me in. My reluctance came from knowing hot, sandy beaches could barely warm the glacial waters of Petit Lake. Women naturally know how to play, how sweet it is when we take time to remember.

We created one scene that has stayed with me like it happened an hour ago. Kathleen, Diana, Lauren and I lined up our chairs on the beach so our feet dangled in the water. We soaked up the sun and warmed our hearts with the trivial talk of women's play. We passed a chunk of new clay from one to the other and each pinched off a piece. While we spoke of women's Moon-times, our menses, and what to do when it starts or stops, we kneaded our clay and punched out womb bowls with our thumbs. Our clay bowls were molded as we talked from our power centers, from our wombs. It was such a womanly thing it blew us all away. In those most joyous peak moments and in breathtakingly beautiful surroundings, I felt real peace and harmony penetrate my bone marrow. We were so contented and relaxed and our hearts were so satisfied, that no serious thoughts found us all day. In the summer of our lives, South on the Medicine Wheel symbolizes the archetype of the life space where childhood grows up. We splashed water and talked about all ages at once.

That night, our Moon Lodge gathering was serendipitous. Steeped in indigenous lore, we watched grandmother Moon named for July, the Strong Sun Moon, rise in all her fullness from the East. As the talking piece went around and around, we each shared myths and true stories about women's sacred relationship to Grandmother Moon and the 28 day cycle women share with her. With Lauren's voice hesitation, Kathleen made a breakthrough. As she fought back tears over the issue of trust, Lauren the icicle draped Sego Lily, warmed up slowly. She had been extremely scared to be out there in the woods, alone with us. During our play day, she relaxed and discovered we were worthy of her trust. When the talking stick came back around the fourth time, Lauren finally gave in and shared more than her usual, "I don't know." Once her fear was exposed, she dropped her guard and allowed her tears to flow. Such a powerful breakthrough caused the rest of us to shed tears of joy and relief. After Lauren cried, she was different and she knew it. When her turn came again, we saw her change. This was the first sign that the caterpillar would turn into a butterfly. She cleared her sniffles and raised her chin so the Divine Feminine could claim her as a woman-becoming. When she spoke, her voice was full of power, because hesitancy had dissolved. Moon Lodges make miracles possible and through the centuries, women have used them to gather personal power through solitude and spiritual practices.

In earth-based cultures, at the first sign of blood from each woman-becoming, girls were separated from the rest of the village and from all activities. During the momentous time of their life when the sacred symbol of womanhood first appeared, girls were given the opportunity to listen and learn from the spiritual messages that streamed through their intuitions. That is the true meaning of a Moon Lodge—when one or more young women take quiet reflective time because their womb blood is flowing. Today, women who are physically and spiritually connected often bleed synchronistically as their primal sisters did all through time. As long as the women of the circle are deeply reassuring and nurturing at this time, the personal wisdom received by each young woman can be prophetic, reassuring, profound, awakening and filled with guidance. Each young woman should have a circle made up of women who will take the time to instruct her about her Moon-time on the deepest levels. Month after month, girls need time to be open to spirit, to be quietly introspective so they can listen to the voice of spirit.

If all components of self are considered equally, adulthood is reached when the body is fully developed and meets up simultaneously with a fully mature mind and spirit. All three—body, mind, and spirit—come together with emotions in each maturing woman. Puberty Rites should be celebrated as the first of many steps on the way to adulthood. Ritual is the one gift from relations that will encourage a girl's maturation. Simple Moon-time habits of silence to consider her developing body and seclusion for her expanding spirit will serve a woman her whole life long.

† † †

After a pleasant fireside breakfast, Kathleen finished her Medicine Wheel teachings. In the West direction, we had already felt the brave drama explode fear and make space for trust and love. When Kathleen connected West to the time when an adolescent grows into adulthood, Lauren listened carefully. Through Autumn's shield, emotions interact with creativity, events and people. In the North, as adults, we spend decades taking care of others younger and older until the snow appears on the top of our heads. Each of us might turn all around this Wheel in a single day, but we can always locate inner stillness in the North-East

where our Wise One observes from her ancient place. Just on the edge
of the rising sun, the Elder Self surveys all the phases and seasons of her
life. The Medicine Wheel symbolizes our life path as it turns around
the seasons.

We moved to a serene inner landscape where our hearts and souls
could luxuriate in the tipi. Kathleen had a treat for us, power dolls. She
presented each of us with a stuffed muslin doll ready to dress, decorate
and own. We agreed to work in silence, so our attention shifted to the
craft materials and the quiet of creativity. We fell into a meditative
mood while we transformed those power dolls into our inner likeness.
After we filled up with silence, we showed our dolls to each other and
talked about each little symbolic part. Symbols are gifts from our subconscious minds and provide ways of knowing which compliment linear
thinking. While she made her doll, Lauren had listened to her inner
wisdom and sorted through what she had already learned about womanhood. Lauren fashioned her doll into a form of herself as a woman
warrior, her mythological heroine ready to triumph on a present-future
journey. She joined our dialogue, voicing her own symbols and beliefs.
At the gateway to her future self, the button on her mouth was both
wide open and closed shut. As she learned to use silence, new experiences urged her to find power in her voice and to shape a worthy identity. While the multitude of voices inside exploded with messages, she
infused her power doll with courage and strength. Lauren began to
dream herself into being.

Diana, Kathleen and I realized how much Lauren was our teacher. In
our spiritual silence, we connected to journeys from birth to age thirteen
and revisited our tremendous growth from age thirteen to fifty.
Although we had not expected a deep shift, we were each thrown back
into our own adolescence. Right there with Lauren, we felt the freshness of being thirteen years old. Cumulative wounds that showed in our
faces, demanded reconciliation. Diana had completely re-experienced
her silent self and still longed for expression. I re-birthed my peerless
adolescent solitude and reveled in the simple joy of my friends. My doll
revealed my future, free to be as primal as the natural history of woman-

hood. Kathleen had grown worldly and queenly, her regal self so vulnerable but undeniably powerful. If there ever was a bridge for generations to meet, dissolve differences and become true playmates, our charming dolls provided that link. We were delighted that our perspectives changed so dramatically when we re-entered that adolescent world. Rites of Passage journeys provide equally marvelous opportunities for women as for girls. Heart messages flowed from our eyes, full of safe and trusted love and void of judgment. What more do women want in relationship with each other or with anyone for that matter?

♦ ♦ ♦

We woke to the dawn chorus and felt the support of accumulated events. Waves of mental images move like pond ripples, out into our personal relationship circle. We demonstrated a mentor's circle to diagram woman's basic needs and how to get them met. For Lauren's first mentor circle, we offered her eight simple needs—money, relationships, body health, school, womanhood, sex, spirituality and play in nature. Inside a simple blank circle, these needs were written on spokes extending from the center. On the line next to each need, we added names of relations and friends who already acted as a mentor to help fulfill those needs. To demonstrate and link with the end of her journey, Lauren chose one of us to mentor play in nature, another for spirituality, and another for womanhood.

We shifted into womanhood training and offered one consummate skill for Lauren's journey. She had a list of words to stimulate women's stories. Through just words, Lauren ventured into our world by asking for stories and definitions from the private lives behind our womanhood. Our tales went on for hours because we shared openly and fearlessly about our experiences of body, psyche, mind and spirit, family, relationships, intuition, women's way of knowing, femininity and men. When she got the hang of the game, this intimate skills training, Lauren mixed up the word list and the order of responders. She received answers and poignant antidotes about creativity, synchronicity, choices, right livelihoods, commitment, community service, resiliency, adversity, passion, mastery, spirituality, rituals, ceremony, dance, motherhood, earth wisdom, yoga and meditation. That's a pretty good list for a start. Since she requested the opposite sex world, we added connections, hopes and dreams, boys and men, patriarchy, sex and making love.

Although Lauren led us into hilarious stories and heard private answers, our real gift to her was the intellectual experience of questioning women. Unearthed by this part of Lauren's sojourn, the roots of womanhood were revealed. We were successful at doing what we wished had been done for us when we were Lauren's age. Not only was she welcomed into our circle, we allowed her to be our witness, also. We were all women-becoming. We filled our need to create special times and places where our growth stages could be celebrated. We focused on the very heart of women's fire, intimacy, the ancient illumination known as *into-me-see*. Women continue to encourage each other to rise above survival, to participate in the juicy elements needed to thrive by taking the time to share stories, laughter, and tears. Together we all experienced Lauren's breakthrough into womanhood's boundless pool of generosity, love, tenderness, non-judgment, trust and healing touches. Those are deep and true womanhood roots, blessings we can share any time.

We shook free the energy of our storytelling adventure and basked in the glow of Lauren's new knowledge. She sensed her initiation crescendo. For mentoring, we used silence again to guide Lauren's three solo experiences. Lauren picked me to mentor play and nature, so with water bottles, power dolls and dogs, we set off. Silence was our only rule. Time in nature is spiritual, so we allowed Earth's harmony to soothe our hearts, minds and souls. Lauren experienced how I use nature to be my mentor, I am a wanderer. In pure play, we delighted in the flowering plants and many animal signs. Feeling joyous and grounded in my body, Lauren and I connected eye to eye, soul to soul and celebrated her peak experience together. The grandmother ancestors moved in and through my thoughts like a weaving shuttle. Because of our silence, we saw wildlife everywhere, even before our dogs did. We returned in a state of pure bliss.

Back in camp, Diana and Kathleen had built the fire, made dinner and transformed the tipi into a sanctuary for Lauren's next solo. After a light dinner, we all painted the face of the woman-becoming for her descent into her dark transformative soul-space. We hoped she would enter her tipi-solo as a caterpillar-adolescent girl and emerge a butterfly-woman. Lauren had chosen Diana to be her spiritual mentor. Together they entered the candle-lit tipi. It was the holy sanctuary where her initiation continued long into the night. They disappeared into mystery. Kathleen and I drummed and sang like the dueling banjos. Diana soothed Lauren and helped her gently drop into deeper peace. She experienced healing touch, massage and a little nap. Diana glowed when she came out of the tipi. Then, Lauren got up filled with energy and danced wildly around her fire. Against the night sky, the candle lit tipi silhouetted Lauren's dancing form while the three of us watched and felt her soaring spirit pull her through the portal of transformation. She danced to our drums for a long time, and when Lauren quieted down, we serenaded her with womanhood lullabies. At midnight, we carefully put out our fire and followed each other down the path for a little sleep.

† † †

To ensure that the morning star would guide her path, we wanted Lauren to be welcomed by the dawn chorus. Like aristocratic grand dames, we painted each other's faces to celebrate Lauren's transformation. When we awakened her and she looked through the lamplight at our painted faces, Lauren laughed at the mirror image of herself. She had chosen Kathleen to be her womanhood mentor, so with blankets, hats, gloves and flashlights, Lauren was led down the threshold path and out into the dew-icy meadow. The pre-dawn skies were streaked with clouds colored purple and orange, then blue and pink. Summer songbirds heralded the dawn, majestic with simultaneous sun rise and moon set. Lauren's premier moment was cosmic and conclusive.

When Kathleen came down the threshold path with Lauren, we lit the party candles to illuminate the banquet of fruit. As we formed a circle and offered our thanksgiving, Lauren's long silence was about to shatter. Her secret poured out like a screaming whisper, "I feel different, and I've been waiting to tell you my spirit name is Dream Dancer." We peered over our breakfast plates into each other's eyes and knew the paradigm had shifted. Our efforts had been successful. I said, "Lauren, when the three of us look at you, we see a woman, so my dear Dream Dancer, welcome to womanhood." We wept joyful tears, circled into one big hug, and welcomed Lauren as a new woman.

♀ ♀ ♀

We love the grandness of finales. In anticipation of Geri's return, we prepared for Lauren's closing ceremony. Standing around the center table of the kitchen tent, Lauren and I connected her first and last journey days. We made feast food and I listened to Lauren's nighttime-dreamtime story of her initiation. She said she had descended into the earth and had come out again. Her soul had dropped down into the dark underworld as had Persephone's, and she returned to the light of day as Lauren the woman who answered the call of Demeter. The myth must have come from her genes, for we had not mentioned it. She will carry Persephone with her and gift the same descent and rebirth to her own daughters.

When a girl is welcomed into a group as a woman, something magical happens to her spirit. Suddenly, her physical being feels as if it belongs. In such a short time, Lauren was transformed from a shy and withholding girl into a gregarious, spirited, and confident woman. I was amazed at her changes. For cognition, she had created neuro-pathways to receive women's ways of knowing, of doing and of being. When she learned to speak her truth, where her fears were met with tears, Lauren realized that trust demanded her to be real. Standing beside me in the kitchen tent, she was wide open to all the connecting points women use to build relationships.

Geri's car pulled up nearby and two of Lauren's siblings raced into camp, Rachel was eleven years old and Jacqueline was just five. With easy grace, Geri resumed her nurturing role as mother to welcome Lauren into womanhood. In the quiet privacy of their tent area, Geri helped Lauren bath and dress, ritually, as suggested from deep within her feminine genome. Women hold those genes of ceremony from prehistory. We look and wait for special moments to activate our old wisdom. Lauren had much to tell about her week in the woods with three wise women. Still to come were preparations for Lauren's ceremony, so she could assume her role as a fully accepted and responsible woman. Her witnesses had arrived, and soon she could take this new role back into her ordinary world.

Except for the caked-on dirt, getting cleaned-up in the woods is easy. It's simply divine to strip naked in the wild and wash in a solar shower. With the return of our men—my partner and Kath's and Diana's—as guests for the closing feast, excitement continued to mount. While we dressed, curious Rachel and Jacqui blended timidity and boldness to peek around trees and behind tents to get to know Lauren's women friends. With their senses alert, they visited each of the mentors in turn, Diana, Kathleen, then me. Both young girls were thrilled to be carried along by our high wave of enthusiasm.

In the spirit of freedom, we gave Lauren her first important womanly choice. We had greeted the three men when they arrived, but they were invited only to our feast celebration. Lauren had decided that she wanted her closing ceremony to mirror the beginning, exclusively in the company of women. We were all dressed in our fancy best and put beautiful wreaths of wildflowers in our hair. With the spotlight of honor on Lauren, the mystery of her transformation was safely returned to the ether. She had been initiated during the night when her soul descended to the dark underworld and returned in the light of day. Young Dream Dancer blossomed in her elaborately guided ceremony, blessed by Kathleen.

Lauren's closing ceremony was presented so her family would see Lauren's transformation. Standing in a circle around the Medicine Wheel, Geri, Rachel and Jacquelyn heard how Lauren had changed. They saw her graceful steps and heard her strong voice. They all gifted Lauren, the woman, with precious things to help her remember. Rachel began a little story, but Diana had to rescue the sobbing girl and finish the reading for her. We all dried each other's tears, gently, like women have always done. As witnesses to the blessings of separations that invigorate relationships, we heard the divine joy of women's love expressed in the reunion. Although we always define ourselves through relationships, we each stand with our feet planted on the Earth, alone with our planet. To complete that beautiful symbolism, with tears in her eyes, Lauren gifted Diana, Kathleen and me with Sand-dollars, plenty so we could each break open one of the perfect circle shells and see the white doves nested inside.

* * *

Here are *End Notes* so this story can end. As with any intention to meet our Higher Selves, this journey culminated with breakthroughs and invisible transformations. We circled back to claim ancient ways and make a difference in Lauren's bloom. As women accept responsibility for bringing up the next generation, we are mindful that young women need healing tools and much more shared wisdom. Initiations can be potent catalysts of motivation. If adults don't provide them, young people will continue to initiate each other through dares. Any guided journey to strive for adulthood is preferable to the hazards of sex, drugs and alcohol abuse. Remember, there are many ways to separate, cross the threshold on a journey, enter the dark night of the soul, awaken, celebrate and reincorporate changes.

With a powerful initiation into womanhood, we realized that change would be carried forward through Lauren. Every girl should have Puberty Rites so that her first step to womanhood is honored. My big question is how to make that possible for all girls. Lauren was introduced to the ways of women in the most profound and sacred way we could imagine from our ancient intuitions, augmented by a few real instructions. What we planned for her initiation and transformation rose from our collective experiences and blended with ancient ways. We sought to honor and recover the adult initiations from our ancestors, the grandmothers of the hunters and gatherers. Lauren's last step to womanhood comes when she's fully fledged, when she leaves her parents home. More than likely, the women around her will make it ceremonious.

For all the next steps to womanhood, girls' needs continue to expand. To create a new women's story in order to raise the next generation with less wounds and regrets, I offer the best of my own gathering in the following chapters.

5

Spirit of Play

Laughter is the lightning rod of play, the eroticism of conversation.

—Eva Hoffman

♦ ♦ ♦

Play will pump the spirit of life back into the experience of growing up. If you carefully examine girls' need, you will see that play fulfills most of them. Still, play is too often viewed as an indulgence. For the hand and mind to learn skilled coordination, adolescents need to build and create things. To learn, they need to make mistakes. They must sample life's variety, while they learn about the Earth and how to care for the planet. All of these needs could be fulfilled by play, but they are often left unfulfilled. The high level of adolescent violence speaks to unmet needs, but if enough of us become players, perhaps the culture will shift back to play.

Even at the start of late childhood, girls still need to be girls. Those of us who were raised to be busy fill our days to overflowing, and unless we are careful, we will raise another generation with our busyness mantra. Play is even more imperative for both girls and those mothers who fill every moment with dance, music and athletics. Fred Donaldson's language takes us to the heart of play, through words like wonder, awe and mystery. "Play practice means keeping in touch with the people and problems encountered in everyday life, while feeling the wonder of it all, experiencing the awe and exploring without losing the mystery." Love, kindness, interconnection, energy, unity, surprise and belonging are all feelings of play which can jolt our memories. As Joe Meeker lovingly did for me, I invite you to simply ponder play. Do you remember times when your inner and outer parts blended harmoniously and magically? What is your personal play history?

Mothers, grandmothers, muses and mentors should discover or reclaim pure play and discuss spirituality and play with young girls. A deep relationship between play with spirituality and spirituality with play builds and continues throughout our lives. Women serve the younger generations best by offering trust and love born out of play. Our peak spiritual experiences spring from those two sacred emotions.

From that heart place called *generativity*, several women helped me sponsor a day-camp for girls eight to fourteen called *Play in Nature*. We offered ten girls a two-week excursion into Nature to play. We asked each camp candidate about their summer plans. If they responded that they had no plans at all, no camps, no vacations, simply no plans, we invited them to come to our play camp free of charge.

The experience of playing in Nature changed all of us. During the first week, all of our play was organized, which actually inhibited playfulness. In between meals and circles, play activities were continuously offered. Scavenger hunt adventures, hikes, crafts under tarps in the rain—all of our activities were equally playful both weeks. During the second week, when we foraged for edible and medicinal plants and went rock climbing, the girls finally allowed their authenticity to come out to play, too. Trust and abundance softened their competitive edges and, with their judgments suspended, real play crept into their experiences. Their laughter became constant because the language of care, kindness, trust and love were present. We were able to play with each other because we trusted one another. When love and trust merge, the spirit of play becomes anchored in our hearts. Playing takes us beyond good mental health, because our spiritual experiences are deepened. Other significant facets of play are freedom, creativity, flow, aliveness, and the temporary suspension of our problems.

Thích Nhât Hanh calls a playful attitude "mindful living and loving." Play is a joyful way to wake up. When life's patterns loom large in our reflection, but we want to move forward, we can call on wisdom to sift through and transform our belief systems. To raise the next generation prepared for life, girls must be spiritually aware and connected in relationship to all aspects of themselves—the mind, body, emotions, and spirit. Each day, girls need to be rewarded with relationships that call forth the fullness of their potential. We find our essence once we discover our personal definition of spirituality, and we continue to move toward spiritual wholeness. Teach girls to use quiet time and to look inside themselves to understand their questions. In quiet, they will find their answers. In the stillness of Nature, where the animals play hide and seek, women enhance our essential natures.

In the wonder of living, we unlock the secrets that provide health and well-being as we learn what appeals to our humanness. What offers the dearest relational and spiritual connections for you? As we unravel the parts of play and thriving, we discover spirit. Both play and spirituality are closely related to thriving. As a sage of the middle-late 20th Century, Joseph Campbell predicted, where spirituality, play and thriving are all woven together, we will find our bliss. In being human, we want to move steadily toward bliss. If we talk about bliss to girls, perhaps they will understand one of life's goals at a younger age than we did. Eventually, we all glimpse bliss, find it elusive, then glimpse it again. Bliss is something we may play hide-and-seek with because it's not a steady state. Otherwise, we would not follow our bliss and it would be called something else. The more playful our spirit, the closer we are to bliss.

Spirituality is known by mystics as "aliveness." Through original play, more aliveness, vitality, and joyous rapture are all possible. Perhaps play reintroduced will encourage a transformation. We will hear invitations to play when we listen with our hearts. Play helps humans evolve, but without play, there is risk of devolution. The surprise of the Universe is that play is necessary to reach our full potential of wholeness. Play interconnects with spirituality through our deepest emotions and both work in unison to build and bond relationships.

Watch what happens when girls grow a little older. Just a moment of reflection on the cultural forces in power produces a profound vision. For the spirit of play to thrive, something has to propel a complete paradigm shift. Play is tough to defend when the ethic of seriousness is hovering, especially given a cultural precedent as demanding as progress. Pure play has more problems in the culture because in most work ethics, play is relegated to leisure. Girls who are uproariously playful between ages eight and ten, can still be doomed by seriousness as young as eleven years old.

Our brains and body skills are dependent on the training we experience during play. Human bodies are rarely tested to their capacities. Gradually and gently, we need to encourage play because it has a direct relation to girls' fullest potential. Women can easily adopt a child-rearing language of care, kindness and love as they integrate play. Such poetic words are not usually used in serious discussions about girls' development. In this culture, when children reach the cusp of adolescence, play is used as a behavioral reward and punishment system, rather than as the means to further cognitive development. Poor play! Real play, filled with creative flow, should inspire the whole decade, eight to eighteen and beyond.

† † †

Many of us, myself included, inherited a work ethic. Parents and teachers prepared me for future work in serious and profitable careers. For people raised with a strong work ethic, our imperative toward cultural progress never included the spirit of play. Play was absent through long years of living. Time to play was earned or relegated to that never-never place of later, when we finished the work. Together progress and our work ethic created a closed feedback loop, there was always more work to be done.

In our culture, play is sanctioned only if it matches the philosophy of competition. This is often the first place girls meet the dominant culture and patriarchal values. All organized sports that teach win-lose at all costs, associate best efforts with competition. Our major sports of baseball, basketball, soccer, golf and football have been wildly successful in the last fifty years. In truth, the patriarchal and dominant attitude of competition has perverted pure and original play. The aggression and competition of major sports have misguided fans about the true nature and values of play.

For women who work and perhaps work too much, play is often postponed until the nest is emptied and the children are launched into their own lives. By the time play becomes a possibility, it seems foreign. Likened to retirement, play is something reserved for later. If I stop to think what is missing in this progressive world, two major things surface. The first is the feminine essence for care—care for everything and everybody, and, second, the playful attitude that leads to joy. Those are crucial ingredients for love. We were once young, carefree, trusting of everything, and in love with the play that made life so interesting. Now we need to call those experiences up from our memories, even though they seem so remote.

Along with the action of pure play, our hearts and our spirits spring to life by the attitude of play, winding around joy and delight. Global researcher and physician, Stuart Brown has documented the origins of play. Play is one of the oldest concepts, because all mammals play. To play is instinctual and primal. It develops skills, relationships and brains. Some of what women have always known about play may just need to be remembered for our girls' well-being.

Play stimulates our brains and furthers our development, but few people actually think of play in these terms. The cerebellum is activated as an alert by the arousal of play, but the arousal is neither terror nor boredom. With the transfer of information from the cerebellum to the neo-cortex, an empowered exchange creates the development of intellect and motor skills. Skills are intensified through the tension that happens when mind and muscle are stimulated. All childhood play contributes to our ability to achieve maturity. Evolution has created the mechanism of play to encourage development.

Stuart Brown taught me an element of play that stuck. Any time our souls become lethargic or bored, our minds and bodies lose sharp coordination, which retards development. Called developmental cessation, this apathy may be rekindled with a regular infusion of play. Just knowing that may renew an adult passion for play. Through the potential in play, any time we are stunted, stuck, stymied or stagnant, play will provide the jump-start.

To complete our view of play, we need to understand there are many different kinds of play: solitary play, group play, creative play, girl's play, women's play, intergenerational play, interspecies play, object play, celebratory play, and your own kind. It's essential to remember that play flows and is not goal-oriented. Play is a connective pattern for life on earth, it connects humans to each other through trust, safety and love. We know those things must be present for play to be possible.

When girls play in Nature, the amount of energy exchanged is dependent on their level of playfulness. To exchange play with other species, we need to dissolve differences first. This can be simple—we need to use love to relax and soften the differences between us and the Others, then we enter a Nature place as a player. While we sit in watchful wonder, practice love, the opposite of fear and invite animals to be themselves. From children, Fred Donaldson learned how to play with wild animals, he is equally comfortable with both groups. Through play, we are dealing with a mysterious force at the center of life. When aggression is present, there is no play.

Through reflection, we see stories of our lives illuminated with deeper meanings because they were embraced by our most playful attitude. If we resist because we are too old or too mature, mere memory will barely recall the enlightenment of play's passion. Remember though, surrender is the first sign of a personal feeling of spirituality. By resuming play, we will be able to divide our years into two philosophical parts—times without play present and times with play. The spiritual revelation in play lights our fire of enthusiasm and desire. Prior to including play consciously, perhaps we constantly re-prioritized life to accommodate just enough leisure time to refresh our point of view.

With play continuously present, we no longer need to adjust our priorities at all. Just as dread, foreboding, worry and guilt can be carried around, so they can also be dispatched. We can replace those burdens with play.

See if this is true for you. Before I found the spirit of play, even pleasure was elusive. Vacations became less enjoyable and more desperately needed as the years progressed. All of that dissolved in the spirit of play.

When we seek a deeper relationship with the spirit-that-lives-in-all-things, revelations come to us through the spirit of play. Girls need this wisdom about play to survive. When women heal wounds and regrets, play approaches and wags its tail at us. Play is our light at the end of the tunnel and deserves a fresh look.

Neither bliss nor thriving is possible without play. It is especially memorable when the spirit is light enough to be considered playful. Play becomes another way to love. Those who rediscover play may feel as giddy or delirious as small children. That is precisely the point. When we welcome play, we thrive. Our lives dance from bliss to play and back again. Spirituality is aliveness, creativity, peak experiences, bliss and also play. Do we value respect, kindness, gentleness, humor, nurturance and flow? If so, then our playful spirit becomes one of our most prized possessions.

Fred Donaldson suggested something absolutely true about play. If our own philosophy was closer to that of the children, they could teach us. It would bring us as close to spirit as the children are and we would learn something about peak experiences through their ecstasy. For grandmothers, bliss is the remembered experience that spirit is located in children's play. Within play, the truth of Taoist philosophy of being and non-being merge. Play provides a middle ground where dualisms, opposites, soften and dissolve.

I believe that directing love toward all things is very spiritual. With that attitude, self dissolves and we can experience being one with all things. "Play creates an environment in which we drop our shields and share our tender human hearts, which is what we all want in the first place," says Fred Donaldson in his book, *Playing by Heart*. The mind relaxes from the rigors of competition like a palm unfolds from a tightened fist—that is pure play. It provides a different stimulation—an aliveness and a re-balanced perception. I found that play was the teacher I most needed to realign all my relationships, for playfulness gives me a sense of belonging to the whole again.

In play we achieve union when all our microscopic parts are in harmony with the whole. We enter a synergy that allows us to flow with the universe. That dance of life should be forever imprinted on our mind's eye. When we realize we are clay from the earth, we will be open enough to see spiritual unity in all living things. Children are clay too, growing, changing, following their spirits, not to be shaped by adults. For girls to locate their natural genius, they must locate play in Nature and in their own bodies. Explorations will lead to discovery of self and all the gifts every girl holds inside. Each girl arrives on this earth with a seed inside her like an acorn. She has a purpose to discover. Intuitively, she knows she can grow into a mighty oak if the earthly conditions can be located.

A young girl who notices the Spring-green of a fluttering aspen leaf will have her delight anchored to natural experiences. Her rapturous reaction easily replaces the gloom of life with joy. Any release of negativity produces a bodily shift. She wants to repeatedly return to the pure delight in the fluttering of a Spring-green leaf. Something about the relationship of play to love is fundamental to who we are, how we walk this earth life, and even how we grow gracefully with our age. Must women be forever granting ourselves permission to play? Even patriarchal aggressors who compete and dominate were once little babies. When we collect our wisdom, combine and compare it as we do, I hope we discover that we will forever be learning about play. Play is one of those few little words that make everything better.

As parents, grandparents, mentors, and othermothers of the next generation, we all need to demonstrate the reverence for Nature that must be taught to girls. But how do we demonstrate something we may not have? Play begins in our own circles. The answer lies in restoring the spiritual foundations of our relationship to the natural world.

Women and girls occasionally stand in the midst of overwhelming uncertainty and mystery, both within and without. Outer and inner life is not different, both are about mystery and uncertainty. We learn from spirituality that we are one and made from the Earth. What happens to our planet happens to us all, knowing that motivates us to walk lighter and with more respect. Through their own millennia of experiences, the Ancient Ones tried to pass down their own learning. Like children, we had to learn for ourselves. Now we can understand the gifts from ancestral ecology. From Nature, we learn an outpouring of our love will reflect back love through good ideas, inspiration and motivation. Nature will function like a stir-stick for our intuitions. Reverence in Nature and for Nature is the spiritual wonder-and-awe feeling we receive from treating the earth as holy. Reconnection with the earth ultimately affirms that we do belong.

If our quest is to raise the next generation knowing their gifts, enjoying a spiritual relationship with all living things, and being a caretaker of the earth, then we need to teach young people about playing in Nature. When they live with only a minimum of negativity and worry, their energy for joy will increase. Playfully, they will discover the ingredients required to thrive in loving relationships. When we follow our bliss in play, we locate our Nature genius.

6

Genius Rises from the Dirt

One can never consent to creep
when one feels an impulse to soar.

—Helen Keller

🝖 🝖 🝖

On the Wheel of Life, in the earliest days of summer, we are in the company of the spirit of a small child. Can you locate the memory trigger of that age? Can you recollect how you viewed life then? What did your inner landscape look like when you were very young? As for the outer landscape, wasn't the ground close and adults far away? Our memories remind us that the natural world was essential for our growth and happiness. Imagine reaching out your hand to your mother or a friend and getting helped along. At age six or seven, we are meek enough in our power to be pulled through difficulty, but strong enough to allow another to help us. When childhood peaked around ten, do you remember how glorious you were then? Imagine being in the spirit of a child for long enough to remember the wonder and awe of those experiences. When we clearly remember, the wisdom of our Elder-self joins the small child spirit on the Wheel.

Children have fun learning the naturalist method. To be their teachers, however, some adults may have to relearn how to pay attention to our way of being in the world. While there are only two parts to Jon

Young's nature awareness formula, it is the combination that is important. The first component for synchronistic awareness is an increased
alertness through vision, called *owl vision* by Young. Practice seeing
everything in your widest field of vision and be sure to pay attention to
the edges. This stretches and exercises neurological pathways. The
other element is walking deliberately, but softly as a fox. Young wittily
calls this "owl vision with fox walking." It is an easy way to flow with
Universal energy. Wonder and awe in Nature create synchronistic
events, but the first and most important Nature skill is increased awareness. One of the rewards of raised awareness is coincidence. When
coincidences happen and we notice, we have raised our awareness one
step closer to our genius.

Something magical also happens when we practice gratitude. Gratitude elevates our awareness so that we allow the planet, Gaia as a living
being, to enter our senses. To awaken our genius and move toward
thriving, remember the ancient practice of gratitude. We often accept
Nature's gifts without acknowledgment. When whispered words of
gratitude are truly felt and carried with heart energy as a give-away from
our spirit, the land we call home, Gaia, receives our gift. This practice
of offering gratitude increases sensory inputs that we receive from the
natural world. Many girls' multi-sensory systems are overloaded with
technological devices. Through naturalist mentoring in just one and
two generations, we will experience a softening and blending of two
cultures, current pop culture with all its technology and the sensuality of
natural women's circles. Where technology takes girls out of their
earthy world, a whole circle of women need to guide their young spirits
back into balance. We can teach children simple methods to rebalance
their bodies and minds so that they can depend on Nature to relocate
their humanness.

Think of energy exchanges as the most ancient of all relationship
secrets. By giving gratitude, we become receptive to all the natural
world offers in return. Give your electronic processing systems a break.
Go to Nature in gratitude in order to prevent malfunction in your internal circuitry. Relax as your imagination sings a melody with Nature.

Perception is the sensual absorption of the world as it enters into a harmonious union with our human energy systems. Nature's tonic to our electronic connections is important to health and well-being. Up to age eighteen, when the most actively creative learning takes place, imagination is ignited by the complexity of Nature from which all later creative activities evolve.

The true genius that we were all born with is located in dirt time even though only a few youngsters actually meet their genius. Dirt time is the amount of time spent with the earthy Earth, playing, dreaming, watching, imagining, sitting and noticing the planet's inhabitants—plants and animals alike. Many people believe each one of us is born with genius capabilities, among them are James Hillman, Clarisa Pinkola Estés, Carolyn Myss, Gary Nabham, and Edith Cobb. For a more convincing argument, review the works of these eminent thinkers.

Naturalist training builds skills in sensory awareness, plant and animal identification, as well as storytelling, journaling and mapping. Questioning by parents and mentors will encourage girls to ask more questions. Curiosity will lead to all the different kingdoms—mammals, plants, trees, birds, reptiles, insects and amphibians. This whole world of brain development is not far from your front door. Genius can be stirred to life out there in Nature. I have long been convinced that genius goes dormant in almost every little human being shortly after they cross the threshold of Late Childhood. Children raised native to their natural world have the best opportunity to keep their genius awake. Nature is the best genius-tutor for girls, through great discoveries everyday, their genius capabilities are stimulated and encouraged. Playing outdoors and experiencing the earth expands and trains young brains.

I borrowed the phrase "dirt time" from the naturalist-tracker Jon Young. Then I blended dirt time with the genius theory carefully developed by Edith Cobb in *The Ecology of Imagination in Childhood*. Through personal interviews, Edith explored the creativity and maturity of people who had tapped into their genius. They all had early childhood experiences in nature that others had missed. In tandem, she watched children through their lens of imagination. Day by day, they developed magical, spiritual relationships in Nature. Our genius is discovered through deeply immersed interactions with Nature and vivid, sensuous imaginations. If we use our imagination as the key to unlock the outdoors, we will simultaneously unlock the mystery of our creative genius. Girls whose imaginations are freed and regularly quickened and challenged by the exploration of the natural world will keep the mystical door to their genius open. I can easily imagine the impact a generation of girl genius-naturalists might have on the planet.

Margaret Mead credited Edith Cobb's thorough interdisciplinary work with the discovery of the natural genius theory. Edith's conclusions came from strands woven together, in-depth interviews with men of genius and decades of watching young children play. She interviewed no women simply because women were rarely recognized as genius in the 1950s and 60s. If genius is a measure for women, very young girls hold all our hope for future geniuses.

We are each born with a genius. As a developmental step, our inherent genius emerges simultaneously with childhood. However, because we have a genius inside doesn't mean we are fulfilled as a genius. The exposure and creation of our genius appears simple—wonder and awe repeated out in Nature blended with imagination—too easy, yet it is so often dismissed. Ultra modern parents have turned to organized activities, especially sports, as a means to stretch and develop their children. You already know all the good things about team sports like soccer, volley ball, or baseball. Girls learn body coordination, team skills, socialization, and competitiveness. Those things do help young women endure the patriarchal world of power, force and control. If unbalanced, this can be costly in the long run. A girl's inner genius needs the wonder and awe of Nature and hundreds of connected moments of discovery and adventure for her highest potential to shine forth. Sports are wonderful for what they contribute to girls' sense of self. Perhaps alone, they are limited to the realm of competitive successes.

Imaginative subjects created in a child's mind help them tap into their creative genius. Imagination is a fundamental intelligence in children's development, which leads to a lifetime of elasticity. Edith Cobb recognized that early experiences of imagination validated and enriched one's imagination. In her research, she discovered imaginary friends during childhood became lifelong companions and guides who reappeared throughout life. Specifically, the seed for a deep and transcendent thinking capacity generates an ability to go beyond the self, which in turn generates a responsive quality in the child's relationship to Nature. Prolonged time in Nature during late childhood produces imaginations of genius quality. Cobb encourages us to read Nature poetically and compassionately so that we may participate in co-creation. Our lives need *interdisciplinarities*, as she called them, varieties for our imaginations to feed upon. Cobb reported that children who've had psychologically or spiritually impactful experiences in Nature draw on those moments all through their lives. Deep Nature experiences are the breath of life for the future of the world. Any child or early adolescent is simply deprived unless she discovers her imagination and inspiration in Nature. Experiences inspired by Nature reshape our perceptions.

Edith Cobb explained that our genius needs only two things: Nature as the fundamental context for childhood experiences and a memory to access the imaginative spark born in childhood. Then our genius will act as a glowing ember and leap into flame. Edith Cobb's central theory is simple—the experience of genius could become common. Despite that fact, presently, the waste of creativity is our norm.

♦ ♦ ♦

Think of Nature as supplemental learning. When a girl first learns how to ask questions, the natural process leads to discoveries and more questions, that signals a moment of her awakening. In the Late Childhood age range of eight to eleven, questions grow more insistent and complex. Each girl needs Coyote Mentoring, that is, she needs her questions turned back on her with bright-eyed directions for locating her answers. This is the age when the lifelong learner is born. When a girl awakens her internal questioner she will become increasingly curious, especially if there is a mother or mentor available to keep the juices flowing. This can be done by pointing the curious girl to Nature, by providing her with field guides and by giving her a corner in a room or the basement to establish a natural history exhibition. Her genius and her wholeness will be discovered in Nature.

Each moment in Nature causes neurons to explode which leads to the development of sensory awareness. Her senses expand her brain patterning, which contributes to her maturity. Whenever we become our own teachers, our love for learning keeps our hearts pumping for more. Curiosity promotes a vitality and aliveness which causes our brains to grow more flexible. Such voluntary learning is more reliable than anything we are forced to learn. Nature is a wonderful and patient teacher with a dramatic element. Predictably, Nature's wow-effect can be counted on to arrest movement. Something quite natural and awesome will attract our attention and cause us to question all over again. You can see how just a bit of Coyote Mentoring, the attentive questioning by an adult, will flip on the switch of inquisitiveness.

Inquisitiveness is one component of genius, the other is imagination. James Hillman, a psychologist whose writings are provocative and insightful, emphasizes psychology as a way of seeing, as a way of imaging and as a way of envisioning being human. He feels most passionate about imaginative soul training for our youth. In *The Soul's Code*, he writes: "...by soul I mean the imaginative possibility in our natures, the experiencing through reflective speculation, dream, image, fantasy—that mode which recognizes all realities as primarily symbolic or metaphorical." Symbolic language is the poetry of the soul. In *Theater of the Imagination, Volume 1 and 2*, Clarissa Pinkola Estés explains the symbolic language of the soul through stories so we might all reclaim understanding of our soul. Her analyses of the gifts in each myth help us remember the gifts we each have inside. The busyness of our culture has separated girls from the language of their soul. Time in nature and stories shared around a circle will stimulate their remembering.

♦ ♦ ♦

Deep within almost every human crisis or drama, the roots of immaturity lie hidden. Violence, drug and alcohol abuse, identity crisis, and
family disruptions are obvious clues. Subtle clues of neurosis are also
plentiful. Psychologically, women's lack of voice, their disempower-
ment, doubt and co-dependence are all prevalent examples of many
women's inabilities to rise above limitations. Instead we remain crushed
by culture and patriarchy which is a sign of our underdeveloped potentials. When we are less than we can be, less than our genetic potential,
our spirits fall easily into crisis.

Given that this is known and reversible, do we offer torment or peace
to our daughters? With training that parents truly hope for, young people can reach their authentic maturity at twenty instead of delaying
maturity until age thirty or forty. Some adults remain stuck in adolescence even longer than mid-life. It's possible to remain stuck until
death. It's also possible to know more about maturity, which is the
achievement of our fullest potentials. When adults finally reach for the
full potential in all of our actions, we will directly affect the well-being
of our planet. Species immaturity and planetary destruction are intri-
cately intertwined. After I read *Nature and Madness* by Paul Shepard, I
borrowed his thesis. A fully mature potential might be possible if
humans were willing to reach across the span of time and reclaim all the
lost wisdom, all the rituals of community and earth-based living, and all
the ways of child-rearing that placed belonging to Nature in a native
context. We have the opportunity, all we need are the awareness and
willingness.

Cognitively, our most valuable brain patterning is created from the
taxonomical collection of information about plant and animal parts and
wholes. Recognizing and naming the Red Winged Blackbird by sight
and sound is a simple example of taxonomy. The same is true for Rob-
ins, for dandelions and for oak trees. Our ancestors evolved these
instinctual genes for learning by naming parts. For a visual analogy,
imagine how a building is constructed. Neurological connectors in one's
brain constructed by detailed collections of information create the spa-
tial framework—like a framed building—for higher intelligence and

awareness. Concretely or literally, neurological connections are made in the first years of life, with abstractions filling in the scaffold details after age twelve. Paul Shepard wrote about the native knowledge youth acquired through the skill of naming the sacred Others. Knowing and naming all the Others clarifies an individual's own identity by knowing what they are not. Laura Namy of Emory University has also been interested in the role of comparison processes for cognitive development. When infants and toddlers first acquire words, an active comparison of two things from the same category facilitates early insight into the category's structure. Luckily, further development of early brain scaffolding can be reconnected and expanded at any time, so raising children actually furthers parents' own development. This intellectual understanding of how our brains make vast stores of knowledge available to us is of particular interest to the baby boomer generation. We have already started to "forget" what we know we know. However, this "it's never too late to grow" theory is also confirmed by the vast cognitive research of Harvard's Kurt Fischer. The classification of birds or plants or animals is an organization system that stimulates maturity through the greatest use of the brain. The identifiers that distinguish Owls from Meadowlarks—the markings, the profiles, the song patterns—all stimulate human brain patterning. Fischer called the patterns, scaffolds. Until neurological connectors are literally built through learning, the plane is level, but can be infinitely built upon when new learning connects to existing scaffolds of knowledge.

If not hampered by culture or teaching methods, our genes have natural urges for learning. Maturity is propelled by such urges for discovery. Successive generations have learned enough to raise the next generation to its fullest developmental potential, but sadly, millions miss both potential and maturity.

♀ ♀ ♀

Cognition develops in Siberia, in Bali, in the Kalahari Desert and in the Himalayas with the same ease. All over the planet, humans have made sense of each unique environment through species naming. Evolution awarded us with capabilities and our great human potential is the prize. Unless culture crushes these innate gifts, naming constructs a mind capable of pursuing a life-long, open-ended adventure through the art of learning that leads to the meaning of meaning.

I have advice for new parents. There is another way, an ancient and forgotten way, to imprint your children with the natural bond of the Earth. You can prepare them for the ecological decisions that their generation will need to make. A fresh look at the old ways promises to give them reverence and respect for the space they share with other natural creatures. Once they achieve this understanding, they can prepare to restore and care for this rare planet. Isn't this something worth offering your children?

From the marrow of their tiny little bones, children are *Homo sapiens*, a highly evolved and adaptable species that once had quite a different lifestyle. For much of the existence of the human species, we were hunter-gatherers. Our children should have rightfully inherited this lifestyle beyond the gap. The gap is the 10,000 year interval of time in which humans created agriculture, cities, domestic animals and all of the problems of the planet the youngest generation have just inherited. Now our children must cope with the ecologically unbalanced, polluted, over-populated and imperiled Earth. The Elders hold these gifts and are now making this offer.

Children can and should have both the technical and the natural worlds at their disposal. After all, they were born into the techno-millennial culture and it continues to be the one in which we live. We Elders have created this world for our children, grandchildren and great-grandchildren to enjoy as we have. Unfortunately, the pressured, fast pace and overwhelming quantity of information, as well as this lifestyle's emphasis on consumerism, causes wide-spread stress and ill-health. If they were born anywhere near the cusp of the Millennium, girls and boys both will come of age distressed to realize that this lifestyle will not provide a sustainable planet for the full length of their lifetime.

Hope is a quality that informs the essence of our being. As the other half of a dualistic tension, despair cosmically dances with hope. Likewise, we assume that recovery is the cosmological partner of loss. While the last centuries have yielded vast cultural losses, to create some healing let's view the whole self—the spirit, mind, and body—as a holistic system inseparable from its parts. Simply put, the female human being, through her current, postmodern development, has also grown to miss most of the natural benefits offered through learning the plant and animal characteristics and uses. Ancient brain patterning has given way to television and the mall crawl. Creative expression through the arts is such fine training for girls' minds, studying the arts rivals Nature for building cognitive patterning. Wonderful and defendable activities like dancing, riding, and sports finely tune girls bodies and helps girls stay present and happy. Think always of balance. For the sake of girls' cognitive future, we must stimulate their interest in nature. Most of the direct benefits of nature immersion echo women's ways of being, the lens of relationships is reflected in the synergy of connectedness. In the whole web of life, everything is related to everything else, and the interrelationships between things, their synergy, combines for a greater result than either one alone.

† † †

Women are exceptionally perceptive and sensitive. We detect energy input from our senses and apply both a conscious and an unconscious interpretation. Our five senses are known collectively as sensory perception. They gather the delectable physical gifts flowing into us through our senses. Unseen energy arrives and is read first by the unconscious mind, which sifts through a storehouse of memories, hopes and fears. When our brain interacts with this energy, a smell or a sound, contact is made between the objective world and the center of our minds. We remain unaware until the information rises to our conscious minds. Because we are primal by genetics, we recognize the smell as skunk and the popping branch as a bounding deer. Each of us can open our collective senses in order to raise our awareness, learning to notice and name each tiny message. This is essential to our communication and connection with each other. Psychiatrist Carl G. Jung proposed that our subconscious minds have access to the collective unconscious, a vast storehouse of wisdom and experience of the whole human race. Our ancestors spent all their lives in Nature, where they evolved primordial senses that we have inherited. We can choose to train our senses for a higher quality of interpersonal communication.

In the quiet of Nature, sitting in our special place with our senses open wide, we can tap into the wisdom of the ages. Sages through time have always revered nature meditation, although sitting quietly is a challenge. First, all the brain chatter from our busy lives must be noticed as the cascading waterfall of constant mind-noise. Then, the chatter needs to be quieted. Only then, our intuition can provide messages about our passion and guide our next steps along the path. Those messages that arrive out of pure and sweet stillness are the divine source finally making contact. See if sitting quietly in Nature holds such rewards for you.

Sight is the main sensory gatherer, because vision collects information from the environment much more efficiently than the other human senses. Sight even bundles the others together into multi-sensory brain impulses. With no hesitation, open all of your senses wide and remember the wonder of being little. From centuries of evolution, your neurons are designed to be receptive to the sensations and astonishments of every part of the world and so it is with your girls. With encouragement to pay close attention to simple physical interactions, girls can become natural enthusiasts of the cosmos. Teach them to sit quietly and feel love for all they experience. Invite them to summon their genius.

Girls' principal developmental foundation for genius is determined by their time in Nature. To expand sensory awareness and brain scaffolding, girls gain two skills by spending time in Nature: First, they watch in silence and second, they learn the names of the creatures and plants in the kingdoms. Lifelong naturalists recognize this as a training, a discipline that involves hours of passionate discovery. When mothers and grandmothers join with girls in the deep exploration of Nature, an understanding of our perceptual abilities begins to grow. In highly evolved child rearing, sensory perception and nature-naming combine with imagination to open the doorway to genius. Nature, our Earth Mother, provides us with everything—the best forum for growth of our collective senses, stimulation to develop elastic imaginations, and she opens the door to our greatest potentials.

Our relationship with Nature bestows equal benefits to our minds and bodies. An enduring and endearing bond with Nature leads to play: pretend play, shape-shifting, animal play, newborns' play. Play is an evolutionary trick that stretches children enabling them to go further and faster. During early childhood, girls are keen on their purely delightful muck-and-mire experiences. Those experiences lay the foundation for understanding the world of controlled thought in later life. Girls will be capable of deeper relationships of heart and mind when adults respond to the youthful, natural desire to be in Nature. Each girl's wholeness depends on this relationship.

When senses are not stimulated in Nature, we all feel lackluster, but this is a developmental disaster for children. Nature creates the best of feelings, just as Nature's absence generates deprivation. Nature is a dependable arena for peak experiences, each one kindles our desire to reach that ecstatic feeling again and again. When any of the sensuous sights, sounds, or smells of Nature enters our senses and stimulates our imaginations, we feel exhilarated. Such beautiful alive feelings help us believe in our own intelligence, excellence and creativity. Anything that overcomes boredom and fear and anger connects to our higher purpose in life. Somehow, we each must overcome the fear of learning and the fear of seeing our own godlike qualities. Women strive for peak experiences as much as adolescent girls do, that enthusiasm lasts a lifetime. Our time spent side-by-side with girls in Nature reclaims some of that original enthusiasm.

♦ ♦ ♦

All children, but especially girls who shy away from science, need to develop one major passion that will take them to Nature. There are many to choose from—painting, drawing and photography top my list of passionate choices. But consider the whole spectrum of things that play on our heart-strings: plants, animals, bugs, butterflies, and birds, to name a few. I have a life-long passion for the photogenic beauty of flowers and also an insatiable quest for edible plants.

What do our passions cause or create? I spend endless hours in the woods photographing what I see and asking so many questions. I find solace in harvesting huckleberries and morels, nettles and plantain. When I return home, I have my rewards. In order to identify any new discoveries, I get busy locating the answers to my questions. To polish my Nature skills, I spend an hour as often as possible just sitting at a vista point and watching life unfold in all directions. Quiet mind meditation is a goal I achieve sometimes, but every time I sit quietly, my senses are stimulated and my imagination wanders freely through every corner of my mind. Sitting with a quiet mind is the main core routine that Jon Young recommends for students of Nature, or naturalists-becoming. Since Nature is constantly in a state of flux, I notice everything new since my last visit to my secret spot and journal about the changes. My sensory skills have developed from this meditation. To quiet the chatter of my mind, I have learned to watch carefully and, for very long moments. The gap between thoughts is where I rest. In the cycle, months flow into seasons, which cascade around the year. Nature skills build brain scaffolding, those inner brain patterns that connect us to our greatest potentials, to our true genius.

Locating passion can be a painful process if girls' inner urgings are sidestepped by someone else's grand design. Each one of us is born with our own grand design. We just need encouragement to be free—free to choose, free to explore, free to imagine. To adults, this may seem a bit messy, but kids can easily spend two days, two weeks or two months on something that tests their level of interest. What frustrates adults is kids' constant re-choosing. Even a brief experience of something allows for elimination—and that's a choice. Both children and adults learn and solve problems daily by moving down to low skill levels and building up new skills to higher levels. Passion is the key to this level of persistence. Children and adults are naturally motivated to master skills by variable repetition. The potential for self-learning and mastery makes knowledge more spontaneous and available. Of all the self-esteem builders, mastering a skill is at the top of the list. The final thrill of girls' creative work is sharing accomplishments with adults. That's why recitals, plays and performances are produced at school. Performances reinforced with passion are remembered and cherished for a lifetime.

✝ ✝ ✝

Let's encourage our girls to imagine themselves at the mastery level for a skill they want to acquire. We can teach them to *think from the end* by observing or reading about mastery in their chosen subject. If you truly remember what it was like to be a little girl or a young woman-becoming, freedom will take you both through a dozen subjects before you stick to one. Your genius may be located at a place where those subjects intersect in a fresh way. This can be useful to people at any age. For example, I quite literally turned 50 before I learned about combining disciplines to create something new. As Edith Cobb and other geniuses have noted, the glorious place where disciplines intersect is described by academics as *interdisciplinarity*. When our imaginations are sufficiently free, the awakening of our genius begins at age eight when the fog of childhood lifts. I am convinced that genius waits there for our own personal awakening.

Creative projects bridge the generation gap with ease and playfulness. The girls need us to be lighter, freer, filled with balanced and harmonious energy. Through awareness we make room for generativity, noticing our feminine energy and the energy of the Divine Feminine. With increased awareness, we can shine the light just where it's most needed.

True maturity has been suppressed by our culture, so we must continually measure ourselves up to our own potentials. Are we ready to be elders in our community and hold a standard for others? Kurt Fischer, a Harvard professor and preeminent researcher on human development, has authored over 200 articles on the development of the brain and adult's struggle for maturity. He has proven that our maturity has been stunted by cultural influences almost beyond our control—consumerism, doing the mall crawl, watching television—these mundane fillers in our life inhibit our imaginations. Television lulls our children's imaginations into a stupor. Until we tap into our natural gifts, our genius, we have unfulfilled potential. Inside each of us lives a genius of desire that tugs at our creativity. That genius potential has a direct connection to our maturity.

Some have called their hearts' desire or longing a *calling* or a *right livelihood*. A calling is a link to our special gifts, our inner genius, our greatest pleasure, and hopefully a source of our income. Everyone has some passion that never truly lets us go. Pass this wisdom onto the girls in your circle. Each one of you has a genius that is part of your genome, your genetic makeup. Awaken your genius as a model for your girl to awaken her genius. Your own motivation can be infectious. Passions are abundantly available and can be reactivated at any age through Nature experiences that expand sensory perceptions and create new brain patterns. We know enough now to help each girl discover her best gifts. If you have been unclear, your own purpose may also be revealed. I believe we can raise the next generation of women to be clear enough about their genius that they learn to listen to the voice of intuition and understand their creative potentials.

Through her stories, Clarissa Estés reintroduced us to the depths of wild woman's imaginations and how to thrive. What does it mean to "thrive?" Very few words have such simplicity. Webster's definition is "to grow and function well," yet there is an allusion that provides more of an impact. Synonyms are "prosper" and "flourish."

How does each woman create a personal formula to thrive? Women—mothers, mentors and, surely, grandmothers—understand that a word like "thrive" means magical things. Perhaps our purpose is to live with exuberance. What would keep the rudder of life so level as to allow for such enthusiasm? Can we cradle the word "thrive" to represent our good intentions? When girls are very young, they do need instructions. Girls' intention to thrive will not be crushed by life if they are taught to listen to their inner selves. From the ages eight to eighteen, girls' wellness is marked by their wonder and awe of the natural world. When we were little, we chased butterflies and watched the ants come and go. Natural wonder became our childhood way to thrive. Expressing our exuberance, we felt long-lasting natural contentment in that world. Through the muse of our memories, we can almost become enthralled again. We are in search of genius, so we must press forward.

♀ ♀ ♀

We have to teach girls that, ecologically, they are a part of the great web of the Earth. They are integral, not separate, from the environment they live in. The natural world opened up and accepted the house you live in, the car you drive and all of your accouterments without as much as a whimper of dissent. The wild once thrived where we now live. Reverence is born in the contemplation of such thoughts.

Instinctually, girls know listening is at the heart of relationships, in particular their relationships with Nature. The feminine essence of Nature is vital, loving, and nurtures the whole of us. We get our sustenance from her efforts, her health, and her energy. Don't be confused about Nature, she is a web that holds life in balance. She is the whole that we find ourselves in when we sit on the Earth and ponder a square yard in front of us.

Ask girls to sit in Nature and look at that tiny space, the square yard right in front of them. Any girl, who sits very quietly for ten minutes, then ten more minutes, will eventually achieve a quiet mind. It is a profound exercise to quiet the mind. Concentration allows both inner and outer landscapes to locate each other. With the accumulation of enough quiet dirt time, the delineation begins to merge the two, inner landscapes made up of heart and mind, spirit and soul, will merge with outer landscapes of Nature, the nearby and the faraway.

The search for self naturally begins at age eight. In late childhood, girls need to be gently led to their awareness. With enough dirt time, their imaginations will wake up their genius. Since humans lost balance in the 20th Century and before, the Millennial Generation can be the first ultra-modern generation to be raised entirely balanced, whole and native to the Earth. If deep Earth relationships can be established between ages eight and ten when the inner voices begin their chatter, girls' foundations of self-esteem and confidence will be anchored to Nature time, a perfect silencer for the inner voices of the critic, the doubter, and the judge. With Earth training and enough dirt time, those inner voices may never quite mature and will be unable to achieve their goal of distraction.

At last there's an antidote for the voices of doom plaguing many women, it's never too late for dirt time. We may find our deepest self-expression in the quiet of our minds, sitting silently in one spot outdoors. I have experienced more personal revelations when I simply sat in silence in a secret spot than at any other time. I have discovered talents I knew nothing about. Every child should have similar opportunities to discover their ecological self. Mitchell Thomashow correctly coined the phrase *ecological identity*. This refers to how people perceive themselves in reference to Nature, as each of us live and breathe in connection to the rhythms of the Earth. When we find ourselves immersed in Nature for solace, processing, or to feel good, we re-learn that experience of Nature serves as a framework for personal decisions, professional choices, and spiritual inquiries. Part of sitting quietly may simply be a spiritual connection to relish the moment, watch how the cycle of the Moon mirrors our personal womanly cycle, or realize how the day fits into the season of the year. When women rediscover how marvelous Nature makes them feel, they should offer that magical serenity to girls.

Do you remember what happens when you take a walk in Nature? First, the freshness of the air and the rush of it into our lungs acts as a diffuser. Aspects of life that have temporarily overwhelmed us quickly diminish in the vibrancy and aliveness in Nature. Our problems can be put into a different perspective on a quiet walk. We can go further with this by consciously turning a simple walk into a walking meditation. This can be done with amazing grace by just emptying the mind of all thoughts. Think empty, so that you leave those thoughts until you are ready to pick them up again. Being a playmate out with the plants and animals of the natural world will prepare women and girls for the next step.

Tools are beginning to add up. With the spirit of play and geniuses about to blossom, all girls need to complete this recipe for thriving is a mentor. Mothers, girls do need a mentor.

7

Generous Mentors' Spirits

If a child is to keep alive her inborn sense of wonder
without any such gift from the fairies, she needs
the companionship of at least one adult who can share it,
rediscovering with her the joy, excitement, and mystery of the world we live
in.

—Rachel Carson

† † †

My friends hold an invisible container for me where I dance and grow. When I am in their company, they show me who I am. Who am I? I am an elder-becoming, seeking ways to connect the generations, seeking ways to be a conduit for ancestral wisdom. I am finally unburdened by emotional baggage. I am loved by friends, family and a wonderful man who is my spiritual partner. Our youth, all the boys and girls on this planet, need us. Those of us from the other generations have created this world, so we have a responsibility to help the youngest generation find their way. We know it is their way to choose and to create. However, the least we can do is acknowledge what we wish had been given to us. We'll begin with what we know.

The resurgence of mentoring is a sign that the collective vision is benefiting from the memories of many people. The unique genome that we each possess has chromosomal markings from 100,000 years ago.

There is much to remember. From the earliest tribes of *Homo sapiens*, our species has used mentoring to pass knowledge from the oldest to the youngest. It is natural for teaching to be passed down from a remembered experience, from the wisdom of our genes. Mentoring is reciprocal, involving equal amounts of giving and receiving. Mentoring wisdom has been passed from tribe to tribe, from country to country. The Chinese Taoists know about mentoring, Native Americans practice it, Kalihari Bushmen use it to this day. Educators have long offered the mentoring process for entry-level teachers, and corporations have tapped into the mentor's feedback loop to boost their sustainability. For the continued evolution of our species and for the development of our children, each woman ought to reach out to mentor a young girl. That is the synergistic loop of knowledge; we learn so much from mirrored relationships and it becomes wisdom when it is shared.

The *mentor's spirit* is a phrase borrowed from Marsha Sinetar. Perhaps auntie, othermother or muse also describes those who have the mentor's spirit. Of the many mentorship qualities, play and trust come first for they are indispensable building blocks for relationships. I set those two qualities in stone, in highly polished granite. For mentored relationships, trust sprouts from the hubris of love and naturally connects to play. Play may be the quality that all occasions can be molded into, like an impression in soft wax. Pure play creates a level playing field for mentors and their mentees where no other rules are needed. Perhaps long ago, mentors introduced elves and fairies to children. The magical people remained part of our lore to inform our intuitions that the spirit of play hovers nearby.

Trust makes play safe and allows love to grow. Combined, they are felt-energies that connect two people's hearts. Alchemically mixed with trust and love, play is an anchor for personal development. Once trust grows through mentoring, the heart feels secure in the alliance of willingness and responsibility. Trustfulness is like something we are certain about, something that is as apparent as seasons that come and go with the movements of the sun, the moon, and the stars.

The girl who is mentored is the essence of mystery. The touch of her soul is delicately expressed when the mentor responds to her silent request for help with her development. She is a woman-to-be who will soon realize the way along the path is fraught with unknowns, maybe even danger. As mentors, we need more than empathy, for we have walked the path from girlhood toward womanhood. We need to be heroines for each other, so that the who-she-is-becoming will be pulled into her bloom. Marsha Sinetar called mentors *shining people*, and said they were those who possess a *self-vanishing* quality. When we provide growth space for a girl, she will soon trust our intentions are life-affirming. With our consistent encouragement and solid support, she will take possession of the center stage of her life, the one and only star of the show.

❦ ❦ ❦

When a mentorship opportunity comes along, embrace it! When she arrives, we know one of the greatest teachers of all has presented herself. Mentoring is different for each situation, and includes all aspects of teaching, but the surprising element is that learning is mutual. Older women have as much to gain from the relationship about insights into life as the pre-teen or teenager. Mentoring is a remembering. When immersed in the company of an adolescent girl, every woman remembers. Teen years are like the glacier that carved the present world—the molding was bumpy along the way, but the final result was sweetly different from the experience. Adolescence is the ground of created, modeled and carved beliefs, which erupts from a fiery core. In mentoring, we are deeply opened to our pure and innocent nature, complete with joy, sorrow and possibilities. Girls need to see how women move beyond our heart blockages. Out of our connections, we will both experience kindness, patience, mindfulness, humility, honesty and other virtues.

Women can open lines of communication with girls and discover the mentor spirit with a little ceremony. In *Meeting at the Crossroads*, Lyn

Brown and Carol Gilligan suggest we take the time to write a letter to our adolescent self. Contrasting the differences and considering the years between our adolescent and adult selves, we will reveal much to ourselves.

If you are a mentor, an othermother, or a muse, you will find it quite an adventure to remember who you were at her age. I invite you to take a memory walk down this friendly nostalgic path. Begin at age eight when you emerged from the dreamy state of childhood. Continue to age ten, a cusp age where you will surely encounter aliveness. Be thorough and take as much time as you need. Write this letter to yourself to discover how you learned the virtues of your soul—empathy, spontaneity, nurturance, harmony and interdependence. Self-understanding depends on core beliefs that were created with an adolescent's mind. For me, this ritual investigation continued several years, lightly and playfully. In searching for the roots of my womanhood, I circled back and discovered my balanced, androgynous self at eleven and twelve so I could resume my relationship with play. The deeper I looked into who I was back then, the happier I became with who I am now. Then I became more present to myself and returned to a thoroughly empowered and happy womanhood. This would be called healing in psychological terms, but really it is simply the glow from our inner person finally connecting to spirit.

Girls have needs that we can best remember by revisiting our spirit-self when we were their age. There is an invisible bond of intimacy between who we were at nine or fifteen years old and our girls at that same age. That bond of intimacy is a key to developing potential and connection through the next years—both theirs and ours. I encourage you to remember your childhood and adolescence because women's original wisdom is located there. Through remembering, we can discover the next rung on our own potential-ladder. There is always another level up, if we continually reach for our highest potential, our girls will too.

When women remember the intimacy we wanted as young girls, our mentor spirits flourish and we will see girls noticing us and reaching up for connection. When we turn on the energy flow, they join us there. Girls are constantly imagining themselves at our age or at least at some future age, either aged eighteen or twenty-one or married with children or single with a career life. Their imaginations are busy, so we can meet them in their imagined world. We can learn that connections are both fantastic and real.

With appropriate awareness, we can locate the girls' brain connection threads—those synapses at the end of each dendrite. We need to meet young people where they think and believe—at every age, every situation, every aspect of life. When women reconnect to youthful life experiences, *her-stories* become lessons learned, valuable wisdom when told around circles for girls. Such moments will present as relief or revelations, as "aha's." That is why learning is equal for mentor and mentee. Those re-connections soothe our psyches and are often healing. A few aha's make the effort of mentorship worthwhile. Mentors become trusted, loyal and passionate advocates who act as a mother/daughter bridge. For both mother and daughter, the mentor offers counsel and support.

Because of the invisible antennas that I have joked about, those ultra-sensitive energy receptors, girls are environmental specialists. Everything in their nearby environment is objectively interpreted, which includes themselves, their peers and the world around them. We don't want to continue to create the contemporary statistics about girls. Women have the ability to offer a hand up and through adolescence, so that girls will not become statistics of a sex-crime, a teen pregnancy, or a suicide. According to the Mainely Girls Study directed by Lyn Mikel Brown, Millennial girls are bugged by the perfect girls shown in the fashion magazines, but inside they are also obsessed with their own definition of a nice girl. The image of a "perfect girl" reflects the masculine-patriarchal objective, she is all body. The nice girl is closer to what each girl is striving towards, a girl who is not at all obsessed with her image. Revealed by the Maine girls in the survey (http://www.mainelygirls.org/), nice girls are "kind and considerate, selfless, they always care, listen, do not hurt others, do not get in trouble, do not express anger directly or publicly, they don't cause scenes, are well behaved, do not feel or at least express sexual desire and are not sexually active. Nice girls try to meet others' expectations, do well in school, are involved in various activities, don't brag or call attention to themselves." The nice girl is what mothers pray about.

The range from nice girl to bad girl is actually very broad. Pushed to recreate their personalities and their degree of tolerance, girls have the ability to cultivate a belligerence that defies common belief. Sometimes they "try on" the language of men and of popular movies, using disgustingly foul street-talk, just to see how it rolls off their tongues and to watch the reaction of their listeners. They are testing their chameleon identities to find out who they are at their core. This testing often challenges mothers and mentors. As long as it's safe, women need to locate themselves back in the days when outrageous behavior belonged to them. This process is called individuating and we all did it. To keep the testing from escalating because of boredom, mentors and mothers can focus on girls' needs. For girls who have circles, the nice girl definition can be thrown in the center to see where everyone connects. Part of women's forgetfulness hinges on their attachment to their own nice girl definition.

After we have reconnected with our adolescent self, we are faced with a burning question: How would our lives have been different if we had the opportunity to experience womanhood with women who taught us what they most wanted to learn themselves? I realize the complexity of this question. A question to close the loop is: What do I wish I had been taught? Through remembering, we re-connect to the girl we were before womanhood. Perhaps we were fragile or tough or a combination of tender toughness. Some of us were happily androgynous at age eight and ten, with an earthiness that came from our relationships with the Earth. Sometimes we had dirt under our fingernails and banged up knees and elbows from falling out of trees. We certainly did not take that personally, we hardly noticed. Then, other times, we could put on tutus and pirouette through the Swan Lake of our own choreography. Do we remember how the difficulties began to mount with each passing year? In her book *The Girl Within*, Emily Hancock interviewed elderly women who remembered age ten as the most vital-alive time of their entire lives.

To discover how women could be more connected to young girls-becoming-women now, I asked over a hundred women in an anonymous, self-addressed, and stamped survey, "Based on what you know now, what do you wish you had known when you were an adolescent?" When each woman looked back to the foundations of her womanhood, they stated regrets that I felt also. I held a personal stake in their answers because they validated my feelings. I then interviewed forty-five of those women who almost unanimously said that however well they were mothered, they needed more support from other women through their adolescent years. Perhaps the road would have been less bumpy, had a mentor pulled me through my self-created suffering.

With or without support, women are continuously called to wholeness, but often we arrive without grace. Grace through adversity is a lesson I have called to myself. What is your main lesson to offer a protégé or a whole circle of women and girls?

♀ ♀ ♀

Adolescent voices are musical, each note and each silent space are equally weighted. Both notes and spaces give depth to the harmony produced from their voices. In the 1980s and 90s, Carol Gilligan led The Girls Project at Harvard University and developed the research on how girls begin to hide their voices at age twelve. Primarily girls hide behind, "I don't know." Narration is a psychological method for telling one's stories, the importance should not be minimized. Circles are the primary places that girls will push through the patriarchal wall that causes them to seek sanctuary by shrinking down into their spirits. For girls to find their voices, they need to be allowed to unravel their stories. The major contribution of mentors is to make sense out of girls' feelings. Patience, empathy, kindness, and even humility are feelings women and girls learn by communicating. These feelings produce a cascading effect—trust to love to feeling safe. Those are the uncomplicated steps to a relationship with an adolescent. Antennas become very useful, when mentors feel and model virtues, girls get it. A beautifully designed and compassionate book about mentor virtues was written by Chungliang Al Huang and Jerry Lynch. Ask your library to get a copy to pass around your circle: *Mentoring: The Tao of Giving and Receiving Wisdom.* A "virtue day" could be a fine distraction for women and girl's circles.

What we call connection, aboriginal Native Americans simply called "the village." Our girls would benefit if we could remember what was known and sacred about child-rearing in those ancient, connected communities. Through girls' lengthy developmental phase and prolonged dependence, their brains need stimulation to create the neurological pathways that must serve them for a lifetime. Native American elders still follow a model that encourages youth to practice skills that ecologically expand brain patterns. Teaching and learning happen naturally through storytelling, journaling, mapping and asking the endless questions of tracking animals through the forest. As described in detail in Gregory Cajete's book, *Look to the Mountain: An Ecology of Indigenous Education,* Elders patiently ask for the evidence, continuously turning kids' questions back around as a test. Girls (and boys, too) consider themselves challenged to demonstrate the skills, and kids often feel helpful when they find answers to the Elders' questions.

It is interesting to notice the similarities in the mentored way of raising children in Nature. Our primal ancestors used brain patterning to prepare for life situations. Through nature mentoring girls receive deep, valued exposure to sustainable practices and useful skills like communications, caretaking and expanding their sensory perceptions. A few remaining primal people still practice mentoring based on thousands of years of experience. The diverse tribes are reclaiming teachings handed down through an oral tradition refined into mythological stories. Around the country there is a grass-roots educational reform blended from these philosophies. Naturalist mentoring mirrors native mentoring, creating strong, elastic and expansive brain patterns, a consequence of studying Nature.

Mentoring reveals major truths. When we were girls, we wanted satisfaction, solutions and clarifications. Without mentoring, girls would still need to reinvent womanhood through their own questions. Girls demand the privilege of asking unlimited questions and receiving unlimited answers. As womanhood is substantially re-invented by each individual, women only need to remember the million details that created our life. When girls are age ten and eleven, they nearly explode with questions. Children who are mentored from late childhood gain life long skills in communication, morality, resilience, values and healthy beliefs. After a few years of mentored practices, the woman-girl partnership grows incredibly strong and the skill level of sixteen year old girls can be simply astonishing. Their courage, competence, confidence and self-esteem come from acquiring useful Nature skills. Through steps that guide each girl toward her maturity, women need to define belonging, mastery, generosity and the grand blueprint of a woman's life of thriving that has been designed on a foundation of interdependence and independence.

♦ ♦ ♦

What about the mentors' questions? What do adolescent girls want and need from women? What are women willing to give? How can two strangers close the circle that connects them? What fundamental differences exist when a woman and a girl mentor each other? What creates the common ground that magnetizes women to girls and girls to women? Can mentored relationships last a decade or more? Is all of life a question?

We won't cease seeking all these answers. Instead we lean on Coyote Mentoring. Ellen Haas and Jon Young elaborated on this way of teaching, which is probably thousands of years old. Mentoring as a Coyote means being a bit of a trickster, which kids love. Instead of answering all their questions, if you respond to them with another question, it puts the search on them. Back in time, when humans initiated every youth into adulthood, elders taught life lessons through questions. Today,

Buddhist monks use *koans*. In our women's circles, Coyote Mentoring will serve us well.

Out in Nature with her protégé, a woman will discover wounds that need to heal from her own adolescence. The mentoring provides such blessed opportunities to examine, reflect and heal. Mentored spirits need only to be cradled with enthusiasm. A young girl wishes to hear that she is wonderful, and she wants her questions encouraged. She cannot be molded, for her spirit is in charge of that project. She can be cradled, supported and inspired. Generativity is the gift of self that middle-aged women give to girls-becoming-women. Angeles Arrien said generativity is the motivation to share wisdom, one generation to another and be the heart cradle for emotional, developmental and spiritual experiences.

♦ ♦ ♦

I waded through these waters with a girl named Dee. She is solely responsible for my passion about mentoring. Through the mirror of our relationship which began in 1996, I have had to face so many of my own issues. I taught her to ask for help, an easy thing for a girl of ten. In group homes and foster homes, she had layers of cultural bandages wrapped around her wounds. This girl so badly wanted to grow up.

So, she asked for a "normal" experience of high school and family life, my husband melted with joy and flinched over the unknown. "She thinks we are normal," we laughed. Dee joined our family when she was seventeen because she had learned that questioning is intertwined around hope. Truly, after all her life experiences, even when her always defiant fourteen year old self surfaces, I am thrilled she has an unspoiled, happy nature. Asking for help isn't easy for Dee, but just imagine how she loves Coyote Mentoring after all these years.

♦ ♦ ♦

A generation happens every 20 years, so locate yourself in the age brackets of 20 to 40, 40 to 60 or true elders. Although the older two generations did not have many techno-electronic gadgets, those we did have lacked the sophistication and the propaganda power of the entertainment industry today. How has the world changed since you were eight or ten years old? Mary Pipher says that no matter what our age now, we wouldn't believe the differences. How are our lives different from the maidens of the Millennium? We might imagine girlhood to be much the same generation after generation. Perhaps that is true until around eight when girls leave the dreamy state of childhood behind. Even for the young girls of today, our imaginations can barely encompass their reality. Try to imagine the intensity of your own adolescent experiences multiplied by a hundred. In *Reviving Ophelia*, Mary Pipher tells us that the last decades have made such a massive difference that our imaginations can't go there. What was innocent, clear and uncomplicated when girls were pre-teen suddenly includes emotions, puberty, the opposite sex, filthy language, oral sex and violence thrust upon girls. They need to be taught by women who are connected to themselves, to the earth and who can envision a balanced life of pop-culture uplifted by a New Story for womanhood. Women must stand ready to demonstrate wholeness while intuiting the ancient Goddess ways of womanhood. Those ways woven into each girl's story will be passed along to the unborns with natural ease.

Mentoring teaches all about relationships, all kinds of relationships. Nature mentoring will take girls outdoors for blessed alone time so they can hear their positive and nurturing inner voices. After all the wise counsel from their woman's circle—from mother, grandmother and their mentor—each girl still needs time alone with the Earth to learn to trust her own counsel. These secret ingredients will surround each girl with a level of protection she needs to thrive.

8

Wrapping the Bundle:
You as Woman

I am a woman, hear me roar
In numbers too big to ignore
And I know too much
To go back and pretend.

—Helen Reddy

⁂

Women must do the deep soul work of unearthing our wounds, of looking deep inside. We used to call this "peeling the onion," because our souls become encased in so many layers of living that they go underground. If we give those places of resistance a new look, along with some fresh light and air, we can begin to forgive. Only when we feel forgiveness for ourselves, can we begin to radiate acceptance and forgiveness out to others. When we have achieved this sense of forgiveness for all the hurts in our lives, then we can reach for maturity once again. Women, do this work best within the safety and love of your dearest friends. When your evolution reaches a new plateau, you will know it. Ask your friends to perform a marvelous and memorable passage ritual to celebrate your transformation!

In reaching for maturity, for our fullest potential, our hearts will open to feel the collective wound. That's where we learn more about love. Through our own suffering, our hearts are broken open in love for one another. I know that's what we want to demonstrate to the young women in circles.

Carolyn Myss coined a phrase that suits these times. She said we must think, do and be "all things simultaneously." Honestly, women just don't need another tall order. Let's wrap this bundle so we can see that she's right. We are women, so our heart-minds can hold it all together. When women—mothers, grandmothers, mentors, muses, and othermothers call a circle and make a long commitment for girls' experience and development, they will discover the mentoring model gives back everything. A women's circle is a balanced, caring, closed system where everything invested comes back to you. Women's circles are the only way we can create a New Story for our culture. That New Story is the blossoming of femininity, the rebirth of the Divine Feminine. For girls to become whole—filled with all the playful vitality of life, capable of becoming the energy of love and radiating light—they must seek balance and consciousness. As Marion Woodman said, only women can bring consciousness to the Great Mother. What does she mean? First, we must hold self-esteem, empowerment, and personal evolution as our highest personal goals. This requires us to come to consciousness for the Divine Feminine. Each of us may have a different answer, for me, I bring consciousness and balance to my busy-ness with dirt time, time to be with my Earth Mother. To be balanced, girls must understand their masculine natures. They will have natural urges to *do* while their feminine natures urge them to *be*. Teach girls to balance these natural urges. When one foot dances for being and one foot dances for doing, our lives are in balance.

† † †

Our relationships hold memories, feelings, and an interdependence so finely woven it can hardly be unraveled. After we respond to *What did you need back then?* our conscious heart-mind emotions blend with memory and imagination. In thoughts, words, and laughter, our whole hearts have been intertwined through our relationships. Thousands of intangibles strengthen the connection we have to each other, encompassing who we are, separately and together, how we differ from each other and how deeply we feel. Those intangibles are energetic connections providing the glue of our relationships. If we want more connections, we make more. If we want fewer, maybe we need to look into the heart of that relationship and ask if it supports our growth.

Clarissa Pinkola Estés suggests we each construct a good story out of our time walking this earth. By telling all the little stories of your life, you gain a mysterious reservoir of personal esteem. Everything in life hinges on your self-esteem, especially women's enigmatic power of intuition. Self-esteem is something gained through the process of action, mistakes, reflection, trust, then more intuited action.

Use your imagination to follow along here. *Be a ripple on your own pond. Breathe deeply and expansively while you connect to the landscape and all Nature. Now, connect to all those mysterious Others seen and unseen, heard and imagined. Nature connections are as real as your inner circle of friends and family. You are connected to this outer landscape, you can come here often. For just a few moments watch how the wind blows across your pond making the flow visible. Wind across water first makes ripples, then gentle waves, then white caps. Softly, the wind becomes a breeze again, then leaves as easily as it came. Notice how your heart beats faster too, when you mirror Nature on your inner landscape. From your mind's eye, your genes are Nature intelligent, so you know what happens when the wind dies down again. Within minutes your pond settles back to its reflective stillness. Serenity returns and the motion of the wind on water retreats to your imagination. Your breath and your heart rate return to a quiet state.*

That visualization took you out to the cosmos to gather the wind and create the white caps, and for a few moments you enjoyed the action. Then the pond returned to stillness. That cosmology connection is as dear as all your other relationships. Everything in this Universe has value. We stand solidly in our place as does the deer in hers and the bear in hers. We all belong. As Dolores LaChapelle, one of the founders of the Deep Ecology Movement would say, we are intrinsically valuable.

Your most dynamic, contentious and revealing relationships are with your family and friends. To learn who you really are inside and to develop personally, you must be reflected through your relations. For the integration of those life lessons and to understand all that you learn from the people in your life, you need time in Nature. With thoughts alone, you ripple out to the pond on your landscape, then on to your bioregion, to your continent and around the world, your thoughts can include the entire planet. Sit quietly in a serene spot while you send your troubles out to the cosmos for a counsel session with the stars or the ancestors. From the spirit of Nature, soothing resolutions and understanding will come back. This is also how you can symbolically connect beyond people to the planetary community. Why would you want to? Organically, this is how you heal and stay in balance. Wholeness comes to you when you sit still in Nature. One day to the next all your quiet moments link together.

Imagine ideas as gossamer threads that weave your life events into a web of relationships. Take recent memories, for example. My story of Lauren's Rites of Passage was recalled from memory for a refreshed connection. As women learn early in our lives, connections are relationships knit together. For each of us, childhood and adolescence created *interdependence* at age eight that grew to be vitally important by age twelve. This is what girls most desire, but they are often afraid to say so. Interdependence is the sacred formula for relationships—all of our moments must create a balance of giving and receiving. One moment you find yourself as a giver, and loving to give; the next moment, you open to receive someone's gift of attention, and you are loving to receive. Interdependence is the intricate, intimate weaving of moments where open-hearted giving and receiving intermingle with each other. Those moments build relationships.

Just as relationships form the basis of our human lives, we see the same is true everywhere in Nature. The outer landscape is elaborately interdependent. Each form, each plant and animal, each leaf on the tree or on the ground, each rabbit-run and fox hole, each creek and river, each knoll and mountain—all of these forms are woven together into the web of life. We need to be empowered to take action to move our declining planet to a state of restored health. There is actually nothing in the world that is not interconnected with us, from a pebble resting at the bottom of the ocean, to the stars of the Milky Way hundreds of light years away. Thich Nhât Hanh named this *interbeing*, for it is the place where we can contemplate and locate our beingness in the pebble or the stars. Interbeing is beautiful chaos where everything is inside everything else. To discover the true nature of interbeing, simply look deeply into the nature of things and practice mindfulness, an alert awareness.

From the moment of birth to the arms of your mother to your first independent steps on the Earth's soil, you are fulfilling your genetic code. As you broaden your perspective over time, the world grows exponentially larger. In the natural world, you form relationships that give birth to your genius, the gifts you carried into this life. Every moment you spend in Nature, even in your own backyard, gives you an experiential base for your growing confidence and your deeper sense of belonging. Interwoven with the interdependence you love about life, you claim your magnificent independence.

Many women grow through adulthood without memories of the steps to awaken their genius. We all have a genius even though we may not become a genius. When we properly grieve the loss of our genius, we can summon her anew to come forth and be the muse we have always needed.

Together, we have imagined how a gathering of women from our own circle might initiate the girls into their Puberty Rites and introduce them into the wondrous world of womanhood. Our true mentor spirit can prevent girls from caving into their resistance. Girls need to hear their own voices to maintain authenticity. We women now need to reflect on all our relationship choices.

♀ ♀ ♀

Your relationship with Self. Relationships take us right into the heart of living and deep intimacy, the *into-me-see* kind of intimacy where we know we are loved unconditionally. It is healthy to notice how we handle all the different relationships in our lives. Our relationship with ourselves is always present. People have all the answers to life's essential questions within them. Listening, fine-tuning and honoring the inner voice will guide us to learn lessons along our life path. We all possess the personal power to generate our own answers, visions, dreams, inner wisdom, and goals can be transformed into our reality. We can construct our lives the way we want.

Your most intimate relationship is the one you have with yourself. Your self is the trinity of mind, body and spirit, each spiced with emotions. To be holistic in your approach, you must perceive wholeness in your multi-faceted beingness to locate your higher wisdom-self. Because your mind is used so much, your self is often identified with the mind or the thoughts that keep you company.

Try switching your focus to your body. It's hard to avoid your body, for your physical being is ever-present. Do a body-scan, all of your parts create a whole. Is your body holy and together? Is your spirit always present? Spirit is described many ways, but your way is the one that counts for you. I like to think of spirit as the breath of my life. When I pay attention to my inhalations and exhalations, my mind is quiet and I know that spirit is with me. That's a simple and profound technique for anyone interested in beginning a practice of meditation. Just follow your breath in and out, think of the molecules of air that come into every cell of your body. Some of that air might have been in Alaska recently, breathed by a moose. Then, think of nothing but your breath.

To improve your relationship with yourself, notice any strains or struggles or fears. Perhaps you only need to think of the self as a whole being, unified both within yourself and in relationship with everything around you. How you relate to yourself is how you relate to all others. Only with honest reflection can you fully consider your separate parts and discover what you need in order to return to wholeness. Think of self-acceptance, integrity, kindness, non-judgment and patience. What do you want? What do you need? Are you in balance and harmony with yourself? Do you need nourishment, a manicure, yoga or meditation? Do you need an hour with Nature or with your journal or both? Every form of nourishment supports the parts that sustain the whole of you. When you feel unified within yourself, then you can focus outside to consider other levels of interactions.

♦ ♦ ♦

Your relationship, Self and Mother. Being a daughter to your mother is the first relationship your self experiences. The depth of your attachment goes beyond the bond of your navel. As we have discovered, separation happens again and again, but your mother provides the clearest mirror for who you are. After all, she witnesses all your ages and stages. She saw you the most, as she watched and guided your growth and development. Have you expanded your intimacy with your mother? Have you the humility to listen to her guidance? Often, the depth of that relationship will be a touchstone for all other relationships. Have you considered how you're connected not just in your heart, but through your thoughts, memories and belief systems.

Until my own Mother passed from this Earth, I didn't understand how deeply our relationship penetrated my conditioning, my whole belief system. I feel a deep empathy for my mother's elderhood and the best of her is kept alive in me. All our relationships are built from the swirling and dancing interconnected systems of heart-mind to memories to beliefs.

Conditioning is a gift from our mothers that will raise our consciousness, challenge our growth, and eventually provide the *aha* of revelation. When we are old, we will know those lessons of growing beyond the likeness of our mothers were the lessons that led to our highest purpose.

♦ ♦ ♦

Your relationship, Self and Peers. Peers, as important others, teach us in a different way than mothers. You first encountered peers over the edges of your stroller. Peers change, sometimes they are friends and sometimes they are not. You play with your friends, those relationships provide a larger arena for your growth and development. As you age, your criteria for friends and peers change. At its broadest, the word "peer" can include best friends and mates and all others. As you grow older, your sisters might enlarge their relationships with you to become your peers as well. Think of all the jouous laughter you have shared with the friends who wanted nothing but gave you all the love you needed.

Elastic perspectives will broaden this category of self with all others. Can you see how your relations are different and yet the same? All of your relationships hold your interest and receive your attention in some way, but you still give a piece of yourself to everyone. People who are on a heart level with you, don't they share a piece of themselves, too? When you hug someone, you blend your body energies for a few moments. Relationships are broad, wide and each one makes us bigger.

† † †

Your sacred relationship, Self and Nature. Your relationship with Nature is a precious and enduring relationship. We can be in touch with the Divine Feminine through our Earth Mother. Your relationship with Nature is always energizing, expansive and true, even if you work constantly and stay indoors most of the time. She is patient and forever holds a place for you to explore, to refresh and to breathe. There is so much complexity that you can never know about it all. If you listen only to inner passions, you could choose a hobby like butterflies, flowers, spiders, birds, snakes, trees or animal tracks, and be fascinated for years. Exploring Nature is one of the easiest hobbies, for it waits patiently for your return. As the most abundant wildlife, birds provide endless fascination. Do you know any birds by their calls? One of my colleagues took me birding for my first time in 1999, and I've been wild about birds ever since. Before then, I didn't know one single bird song!

All of us require more intimacy in our relationship with Nature. Women can rely on Nature for solace when it seems that nothing else can handle our deepest sufferings. Nature offers just the energetic balance for women and girls to discover and nurture their inner feminine selves. Like many modern women, I was conditioned by patriarchy, the power structure that determines the demanding pace of many careers. Career women (like I was for twenty years) wreck adrenals and immune systems by listening to those relentlessly demanding inner voices. After a twenty-year financial career, oh how I needed Nature's solace! What's your level of need?

When women connect inner and outer worlds through quiet time in Nature, our masculine and feminine energies can evolve as they interact with natural energies. That's precisely how we can teach girls to develop consciousness, through our guidance and experience. Each one of us had to find our way through this maze. If women simplify girls' path to womanhood, their genius can rise above the cultural muck. Balanced between archetypal energies, each girl and each women deserves to be freed from her ignorance so her authentic personality can soar in harmony with the Earth.

The beauty of our wild places grows more precious everyday. Looking forward to our grandchildren and great-grandchildren, we all need to become activists to protect Nature for those who are not yet born. In our own bioregion, we need to look for places where abuse has occurred and lend our energies to repair and restore them. Around the neighborhood, damage is often blatant and our help will make a difference. More than any other relationship, the one we display in Nature with our children will be the one they remember. Our young have inherited an abused planet, so their generation will need to face the pertinent facts and supply the restorative energy.

The reasons why you need to lend a hand are not always obvious, although abuses usually are easy to spot. Say to the girls you mentor, "Before you grow into the busiest woman standing next to your mother, take time to sit in Nature."

⁑ ⁑ ⁑

Your relationship, Self and Planet. Earth feeds you, holds you with her gravity, entertains you and absorbs all your negative energy. She soothes your nerves, clears your mind and stimulates your good ideas. And all of that might have happened in a walk around the neighborhood! Your relationship with the planet Earth is a spiritual relationship, because you are kindred spirits. Go quietly into an unspoiled place in Nature with your awareness turned up high. Your energy changes because your sensory inputs are soothed into Nature's own harmonious baseline. You will sense an order and a serenity that transcends even the physical beauty. What the Earth Mother reveals to your senses is the mystery of spiritual consciousness, the very soul of life.

Your relationship with the planet only differs with Nature when you think of wholes. Nature is right outside, when we speak of the Earth or Gaia, we mean the entire globe. Often the whole picture helps you see how your contribution can be beneficial. To understand your kinship with the planet Earth, imagine that she needs your help and has asked you to do some kind act on her behalf. For all the sustenance and support she has provided throughout your life, would you refuse her need?

Women are sensitive to the spirit-in-all-things, which guides the development of our natural genius. In the Earth household, that spirit dwells in plants, animals, stones, dirt, rivers and mountains—in everything. We are concerned about the health of the Earth and its impact on our long-term future. How do we inform the children of the new generation, the Millennial generation, about the ill-health of the Earth that we are passing along to them. They will spend their lives restoring the damaged and unhealthy planet they have inherited. How do we tell them this news?

The blunt truth about the health of our planet is that we have been in the midst of an ecological crisis for some time. Each day, new babies swell the population already here on the earth. With the birth rate still out of control, humans have almost become like locusts. We are devouring the raw materials of the Earth faster that we are replacing them. Long ago, the Iroquois Nation offered a rule for our actions. Before we act, first ask what would be the effect of those actions on seven generations into the future, about 150 years. If you are somewhere in the middle of life as I am, you might be able to envision the full span of seven generations. Add only one "great" onto grandparents, and they come into view. Then add "great" onto grandchildren and the vision of seven full generations is complete. Our women's work, our great give-away should be for the Eighth Generation. With such a give-away, we can unite with a common cause, women's relationship with the planet on behalf of our children's great-grand-children. Now, that is a worthy revolutionary banner, one we can work on quietly within our own circles.

♀ ♀ ♀

As we proceed erratically along the path of modernism, these children could have a wholly different world—a wasteland—to pass to their grandchildren. This Millennial generation has inherited a challenge, unlike any ever experienced in the life of the planet; it is something for which they will need special preparation. Perhaps a year-long project would help them approach the dimension of the truth. Information sets us free. We must motivate the children to salvage their inheritance. While the educational system has been charged with dispensing this information, they should not be responsible for the emotional side of such bad news. The extent of their truths often depends wholly on teachers and their administration. The truth about the health of the planet needs to be investigated fully by each family, shared in communities and in circles. My dear friend and mentor, Susan Morgan is a bright light in the conservation field. She suggested that a project could be designed from an internet search on key-words. We used *ecological activism for kids* and brought up thousands of hits. We both ask only that your children are informed about the state of the world before the consequences catch them emotionally unprepared for the truth. We need to be sensitive to the impact, but stop hiding the whole truth. Our involvement, personal touches, choices for consumption, decisions about production and technology have all lacked a grounded ecological philosophy. We must raise our awareness, find our niche for action, and get to work for the preservation of the Earth.

Some say the hope of the world rests with the next generation, their innocent idealism and their energy for activism. However hopeful, their wisdom is limited. In their early years, adolescents are truly interested in their larger world as much as they are interested in relationships. Introspection is the entry point for the ecological involvement of adolescents in a viable future. From age twelve to fourteen, adolescents begin to widely expand their world-view. Mothers and mentors can suggest that girls do their own discovery, but we can support, watch and lead. They enter through their perspectives, and with Coyote Mentoring we only need to respond with the gentlest of questions. Coyote Mentoring will encourage girls to develop their own beliefs about ecology, about the health of the planet, and how they feel about what they have inherited. If girls are presented with the riddle of what their role should be, they will find reason and cause in the ecological crisis to dig deeper and find out more about it. We provide support for the deep emotions they experience, when their personal investigation reveals the details of the crisis. They will not be as psychologically damaged as the generations just ahead who were either informed casually, callously or not at all.

When women build relationships through all our connecting points, we become stoked and empowered. Underneath all of our relationships is the spirit of us, the spirit that lives in all things. The kind of spirituality that is needed is one that honors our connection to each other. We need to shape a new legacy from the spirit of our connection in relationships so we can break the chain of violence that is passed from one generation to another.

† † †

We begin here. Our planet needs our kindness and our care as desperately as our children do. We of generous spirit need to find out the

truth and stand beside the younger generation with even tighter relationships than other generations have experienced. This younger generation will eventually be angry at their inheritance. Then they will need
us to help them channel that anger into restoration projects and political efforts to turn the tide of wasteful consumerism toward sustainable
use and renewable energy. Women (and men) can come together
through spirituality. Hopefully we will find as much spirituality in the
face of each other as we find in whales, in bird song and in the grace of
a butterfly. Please accept this is an invitation to begin and go where
your spirit takes you.

Millions of us are embracing—or hover on the verge of discovering—our spiritual essence: our intuitiveness, wisdom, resilience, compassion, and our centered-hearts. Women of vision are transforming
the world with the luminous power of spiritual goodness, purpose, and
grace. A rich new external world must spring from our lush interiors.
We must lay a loving foundation for our own hearts and spirits before
we can build soulful communities around us. We won't hear the call of
our spirit if we constantly drown it out with incessant activity. We need
moments of absolute stillness to quiet our mind's chatter and let our
souls stretch and speak to us. Women have cyclical natures, so we need
to turn inward for reflection in order to balance our outer energy and
life. We don't live in a society that rewards quiet time, such as sitting
quietly watching Nature. If you surround yourself with the natural
world, you will find a communion with all the things that want to communicate with you. There's no need to judge that communion; since
you are responding to a real dialogue, you can allow it to continue without interference. You will return home with a special gift tucked inside
your heart. Our spiritual life merges with our everyday life. Spirituality
stems from relationships with other people and your ability to open
your heart to all others. It will require feminine strength and courage to
balance the runaway caricature of masculine values.

I want to understand the language of the prairie, the edge of the sage,
and the willows. I want to relish all the wild Others on this beautiful
Earth. In the second half of life, I have become an advocate of wild-

flowers and of girls, knowing that their ritual initiations are as vital as the urgency of Spring. As a mentor for girls and women's circles, I carefully hold you in my bundle with the spirit of play. I have become a protector of the very web in which we all dance. My Earth Mother often cradles me. I wish the same for you.

I will say leave a good quarter
of the time for feast and celebration
or your soul will die.

—Francois Monnet

APPENDIX A
The Wisdom of Stories

Barchers, S. I. (1990). <u>Wise women: Folk and fairy tales from around the world.</u> Libraries Unlimited.

Deloria, E. (1988). <u>Waterlily.</u> Lincoln, NB: University of Nebraska Press.

Dooling, D. M. (Ed.). 1986). <u>A way of working the spiritual dimension of craft.</u> New York: Parabola.

Estés, C.P. (1992). <u>Women who run with the wolves: Myths and stories of the wild woman archetype.</u> NY: Ballantine.

Estés, C. P. (1992-7). <u>The creative fire; The radiant coat; The boy who married an eagle; The red shoes; Warming the stone child; In the house of the riddle mother; The faithful gardner; Theatre of the imagination, Volume I and II.</u> Audio cassette tapes. Boulder, CO: Sounds True.

Gunn Allen, P. (1991). <u>The sacred hoop: Recovering the feminine in American Indian traditions.</u> Boston: Beacon.

Gunn Allen, P. (1991). <u>Grandmothers of the light: A medicine woman's sourcebook.</u> Boston: Beacon.

Gunn Allen, P. & Clark Smith, P. (1996), <u>As long as the rivers flow: The stories of nine Native Americans.</u> New York: Scholastic Press.

Gunn Allen, P. (1995). <u>Song of the turtle: American Indian literature 1974–1994.</u> New York: Ballantine.

Harrison, J. (1989). <u>The theory and practice of rivers and new poems.</u> Livingston, MT: Clark City Press.

McLain, G. (1990). <u>The Indian way: Learning to communicate with Mother Earth.</u> Sante Fe, NM: John Muir Publication.

Narayan, K. (1997). <u>Mondays on the dark night of the moon: Himalayan foothill folktales.</u> New York: Oxford University Press.

Nelson, R. (1989). <u>The island within.</u> San Francisco: North Point Press.

Niethammer, C. (1977). <u>Daughters of the earth: The lives and legends of American Indian women.</u> NY: Macmillan.

Nerburn, K. & Mengelkoch, L. (1991). <u>Native American wisdom.</u> San Rafael, CA: New World Library.

Prather, H. & Prather, G. (1991). <u>Parables from other planets: Folktales of the Universe.</u> N Y: Bantam Books.

Rosenberg, D. (1996). <u>Folklore, myths, and legends: A world perspective.</u> Lincolnwood, IL: NTC.

Silko, L. M. (1981). <u>Storyteller.</u> New York: Arcade.

Snyder, G. (1957). <u>Earth house hold.</u> New York: New Directions Books.

Snyder, G. (1961). <u>Six sections from Mountains and rivers without end plus one.</u> San F: Four Seasons Foundation.

Snyder, G. (1980). <u>The real work: Interviews & talks 1964–1979.</u> New York: New Directions Books.

Snyder, G. (1990). The practice of the wild. San Francisco: North Point Press.

Snyder, G. (1995). A place in space: Ethics, aesthetics, and watersheds. Washington, D.C.: Counterpoint.

Spretnak, C. (1978) Lost Goddesses of early Greece: A collection of pre-Hellenic myths. Berkeley, Moon Books.

Suzuki, D. & Knudtson, P. (1992). Wisdom of the Elders: Honoring sacred Native visions of Nature. New York: Bantam.

Travers, P. (1994). What the bee knows: Reflections on myth, symbols and story. New York: Viking.

Van Matre, S. & Weiler, B. (1983). The Earth speaks. Warrenville, IL: The Institute for Earth Education.

Walker, B. G. (1996). Feminist fairy tales. San Francisco: HarperSan-Francisco.

Youngs, B. B. (1998). Taste-berry tales: Stories to lift the spirit, fill the heart and feed the soul. Deerfield Beach, FL: Health Communications.

APPENDIX B

Risk List[1]

Risks are the factors that obstruct an adolescent girl's ascendancy into her birthright of a happy, confident, self-assured womanhood (according to Carol Eagle & Carol Colman, 1993). Together the potential risks that adolescents face are so numerous that a list is the best way to display them. Note that several risks belong to different categories simultaneously.

1. Emotional

    Parental Role Model

    Parental Emotional Problems

    Equality at Home

- Depression

    1/3 of girls, 2/3 of women

    Link to 5000 adolescent girl suicides/year

- Low Self-esteem

    Looks

    School transition

    Lack of confidence inhibits skills mastery

    Limits dreams, challenges, aspirations

    Risk of dead-end, low paying jobs

- The Patriarchal Wall

    Gender disparity

    Subtle and not so subtle stereotyping

    Dualism of connectedness and autonomy

- Voice/Silence

    Conceal and deny emotions

    acts "in" blames self

    Risk of lost authenticity

    Risk of lost sense of self

    Voice loss advances to silence by age 16

- Excessive Imitation

    Sense of self development inhibited

    Identity linked to others

- Obsessive Eating Disorders

    Fat phobia

    Anorexia nervosa, list of associated risks

    Bulimia, combined result in 10% deaths

2. Physical

- Early and Late Development

    Specific areas of bodily development

---

1.   Adapted and Expanded by Gail Burkett, PhD March 17, 2001
From Carol J. Eagle and Carol Colman (1993). All That She Can Be: Helping Your Daughter Achieve Her Full Potential and Maintain Her Self-Esteem During the Critical Years of Adolescence. New York: Simon & Schuster.

Trauma from uninformed menses

- Smoking from peer pressure

  500,000 girls new smokers each year

- Drug Use and Abuse

  Earlier ages, lack of cause/effect analysis

- Alcohol Use and Abuse

  Driving impaired

  20% 14–17 are "problem drinkers"

  Both alcohol and drug use

  > abusing parents
  > feelings of worthlessness
  > laissez-faire parenting

- Sex

  Self-esteem

  AIDS, STDs

  500,000 births and 500,000 abortions

  1/3 15 and older girls are sexually active

  1/3 do not use contraception first time

  20% do not use contraceptive devices at all

  > Date Rape
  > Sexual Harassment

3. Self-destructive Behavior

- Unassertive Relationships

  2nd class citizen

  Oppression victim

- Academic Failure

  Too "dumb", low self-esteem

  Low paying jobs, risk welfare

  Unaware that as woman will work 30 years

- Risks from accidents

  Growing cause of death among adolescents

  Dares

- Suicides

  5000 each year

4. Parenting Styles

- Over protective mother

  not street smart

  lacks confidence and skill

- Under protective mother

  Feeling like a "bad person"

  Not worthy of love and attention

  Experiments with sex, drugs,

  Serious trouble

- Competitive mother

  Feels never quite "good enough"

  Engages in destructive behavior

- Stage mother

  Never becomes her own person

  Does not create a life of her own

- Best friend mother

  Develops without sense of self

  Disconnected with what she wants

  Never learns to speak her mind

  Never learns relationship reciprocity

- Over protective father

  Emotional growth thwarted

  Develops a poor sense of self

  Expects men to solve problems for her

- Withdrawn father

  Feels at fault

  Feels unworthy of love

  Feels insecure with other men

- Authoritarian father

  Distorted view of gender roles

  Feels subservient to men

  Feels her opinions are unimportant

- Most wonderful father

  No other man can compete

  Believes love is blind devotion and subservience

- Risks from divorced parents

- Environmental Poverty

References

Prologue

Arrien, Angeles (1992). The four-fold way: Walking the paths of the warrior, teacher, healer and visionary. New York: HarperCollins.

Arrien, Angeles (1998). The second half of life: The blossoming of your creative self. Boulder, CO: Sounds True Audio.

Cobb, Edith (1977). The ecology of imagination in childhood. New York: Columbia University Press.

Chapter One: Dancing with the Ancestors

Cajete, Gregory (1994). Look to the mountain: An ecology of indigenous education. Durango, CO: Kavakí Press.

Cobb, Edith (1977). The ecology of imagination in childhood. New York: Columbia University Press.

Gimbutas, Marija (1989). The language of the Goddess. San Francisco: Harper and Row.

Gimbutas, Marija (1991). The civilization of the Goddess. San Francisco: Harper San Francisco.

Mails, Thomas E. (1988). Secret Native American Pathways: A guide to inner peace. Tulsa, OK: Council Oaks Books.

Medicine Eagle, Brooke (1991). Buffalo Woman comes singing: The spirit song of a rainbow medicine woman. New York: Ballantine Books.

Shepard, Paul (1978). Thinking animals: Animals and the development of human intelligence. New York: Viking Press.

Shepard, Paul (1982). Nature and madness. San Francisco: Sierra Club Books.

Shepard, Paul (1998). Coming home to the Pleistocene. Washington, DC: Island Press.

Chapter Two: Change for the Bliss of Thriving

Allen, Paula Gunn (1985). The sacred hoop: Recovering the feminine in American Indian traditions. Boston: Beacon Press.

Anderson, Lorraine (1991). (Ed.). Sisters of the Earth: Women's prose and poetry about nature. New York: Vintage Books.

Belenky, Mary Field, Blythe McVicker Clinchy, Nancy Rule Goldberger, & Jill Mattuck Tarule (1986). Women's ways of knowing. New York: Basic Books.

Eisler, Riane (1988). The Chalice and The Blade: Our History, Our Future. San Francisco, CA: HarperSanFrancisco.

Eisler, Riane & David Loye (1990). The Partnership Way: New Tools for Living and Learning. New York, NY: HarperCollins.

Hardin, J. Wolf (2000). Chanting home: Recovering sense of place. Sante Fe, NM: SwanRaven.

Shepard, Paul (1998). Coming home to the Pleistocene. Washington, DC: Island Press.

Chapter Three: Girls' Needs

Baldwin, Christina (1994). Calling the Circle : The First and Future Culture. New York: Bantam.

Bolen, Jean Shinoda (1999). The Millionth Circle: How to Change Ourselves and The World—The Essential Guide to Women's Circles. York Beach, ME: Conari Press

Borysenko, Joan (1987) Minding the body, mending the mind. Reading, MA: Addison-Wesley.

Brumberg, Joan Jacobs (1997). The body project: An intimate history of American Girls. New York, NY: Random House.

Christ, Carol P. (1986). Diving deep and surfacing: Women writers on spiritual quest. Boston: Beacon Press.

Debold, Elizabeth, Marie C. Wilson, & Idelisse Malave (1993). Mother-daughter revolution. New York: Addison-Wesley.

Eagle, Carol J. & Carol Colman (1993). All That She Can Be: Helping Your Daughter Achieve Her Full Potential and Maintain Her Self-Esteem During the Critical Years of Adolescence. New York: Simon & Schuster.

Eisler, Raine T. (2000). Tomorrow's Children: A blueprint for partnership education in the 21st Century. Boulder, CO: Westview Press.

Foster, Steven (1989). The book of the vision quest: Personal transformation in the wilderness. New York, NY: Simon and Schuester.

Grahn, Judy (1993). Blood, Bread and Roses: How Menstruation Created the World, Boston: Beacon.

Krall, Florence R. (1994). Ecotone: Wayfaring on the margins. Albany, NY: State University of New York Press.

Quinn, Janet F. (1999). I am a woman finding my voice: Celebrating the extraordinary blessings of being a woman. New York: Eagle Brook.

Rutter, Virginia Bean (1996). Celebrating Girls—Nurturing and Empowering Our Daughters. Berkeley, CA: Conari Press

Rutter, Virginia Bean (2000). Embracing Persephone: How to be the mother you want for the daughter you cherish. New York, NY: Kodansha America.

Schiller, Pam & Tamera Bryant (1999). The Values Book: Teaching 16 basic values to young children. Beltsville, MD: Gryphon House.

Sheehy, Gail (1974). Passages: Predictable Crises of Adult Life. New York: Bantam.

Spretnak, Charlene (1991). States of grace: The recovery of meaning in the Postmodern Age. New York: Harper Collins.

Spretnak, Charlene (1992). Lost Goddesses of early Greece: A collection of pre-Hellenic myths with a new preface. New York: Harper Collins.

Spretnak, Charlene (1999). The resurgence of the real: Body, nature, and place in a hypermodern world. New York: Routledge.

Steinem, Gloria (1983). Outrageous acts and everyday rebellions. New York: Holt, Rinehart, and Winston.

Steinem, Gloria (1992). Revolution from within: A book of self-esteem. Boston: Little, Brown, and Company.

Turner, Victor (1969). The ritual process: structure and anti-structure. Chicago: Aldine Publishing Co

Van Gennep, Arnold (1960). The Rites of Passage. London: Routledge.

Wheatley, Margaret (2002). Turning to one another: Simple conversations to restore hope for the future. SanFrancisco, CA: Barrett-
Koehler Publishers.

Wolfe, Naomi (1997). Promiscuities: The secret struggle for womanhood. New York, NY: Random House.

Chapter Four: Rites of Passage into Womanhood

Brown, Lyn Mikel and Gilligan, Carol (1992) Meeting at the Crossroads: Women's payshology and girls' development. New York:
Ballantine Books.

Bruetsch, Anne, J. Jaffe, M. N. Patterson, & L. Sample, (1996). The
heroic journey: A Rite of Passage program. Tucson, AZ: Zephyr
Press.

Dacey, J. S., & A. J. Packer, (1992). The nurturing parent: How to raise
creative, loving, responsible children. New York: A Fireside Book.

Foster, Stephen & Little, Meredith (1989). A wilderness rite of passage
for youth: A teacher's manual. Big Pine, CA: Rites of Passage
Press.

Foster, Stephen & Little, Meredith (1989). The roaring of the sacred
river: The wilderness quest for vision and self-healing. New York:
Prentice Hall.

Gilligan, Carol, Nona P. Lyons, & Trudi J. Hamner (1990). Making
connections: The relational worlds of adolescent girls at Emma
Willard School. Cambridge, MA: Harvard University Press.

Gilligan, Carol, Annie G. Rogers, & Deborah L. Tolman (1991). Women, Girls & psychotherapy: Framing Resistance. New York: Haworth Press.

Duerk, Judith (1990). Circle of Stones: Woman's journey to herself. Philadelphia, PA Innisfree Press

Duerk, Judith (1993). I sit listening to the wind: Woman's encounter within herself. San Diego, CA: LuraMedia

Gawain, Shakti (1991). Awakening: A daily guide to conscious living. San Rafael, CA: New World Library.

Van Gennep, Arnold (1960). The Rites of Passage. London: Routledge.

Turner, Victor (1969). The ritual process: structure and anti-structure. Chicago: Aldine.

Chapter Five: The Spirit of Play

Brown, Stuart L. (1995). Concepts of childhood and play: An Interview With Brian Sutton-Smith. ReVision, 17(4), 35–42.

Brown, Stuart L. (1995). Through the lens of play. ReVision, 17(4), 4–13.

Brown, Stuart L. (2004). As found on the internet: http://www.instituteforplay.com/13stuart_brown.htm

Campbell, Joseph (1972). The hero with a thousand faces. Princeton, NJ: Princeton University Press.

Donaldson, O. Fred (1993). Playing by heart: The vision and practice of belonging. Deerfield Beach, FL: Health Communications.

Eliade, Michael (1958/1975). Rites and symbols of initiation: The mysteries of birth and rebirth. New York: Harper and Row.

Meeker, Joseph W. (1995). Comedy and a play ethic. ReVision, 17(4), 21–24.

Meeker, Joseph W. (1972). The comedy of survival: In search of an environmental ethic. Los Angeles, CA: Guild of Tutors Press.

Meeker, Joseph W. (2000.2001). Comedy and a play ethic. Whole Terrain, 9, 11–14.

Nhât Hanh, Thích (1997). Teachings on love. Berkeley, CA: Parallax.

Nachmanovitch, Stephen. (1990). Free play: Improvisation in life and art. Los Angeles: Tarcher.

Pipher, Mary (1994). Reviving Ophelia: Saving the selves of adolescent girls, New York: Ballantine.

Chapter Six: Genius Rises From the Dirt

Cobb, Edith (1977). The ecology of imagination in childhood. New York: Columbia University Press.

Fischer, Kurt, Z. Yan and J. Stewart. (2003). Adult Cognitive Development: Dynamics in the Developmental web in Handbook of Developmental Psychology edited by Jaan Valsiner & Kevin Connolly. Sage Publications.

Fischer, Kurt W. (1987). Relations between brain and cognitive development. *Child Development, 58*, 623–632.

Fischer, Kurt W., Bullock, D., Rotenberg, E.J., & Raya, P. (1993). The dynamics of competence: How context contributes directly to skill. In R. Wozniak & K.W. Fischer (Eds.), *Development in context: Acting and thinking in specific environments*. JPS Series on Knowledge and Development. Hillsdale, N.J.: Erlbaum.

Gallegos, E. Stephen (1992). Animals of the four windows: Integrating thinking, sensing, feeling and imagery. Santa Fe, NM: Moon Bear Press.

Hillman, James (1997). The soul's code: In search of character and calling. New York, NY: Warner Books.

Jung, Carl (1964). Man and his symbols. Garden City, NY: Doubleday.

Levoy, Gregg (1997). Callings: Finding and following an authentic life. New York: Harmony Books.

Nabhan, Gary P. & Stephen Trimble (1994) The geography of childhood: Why children need wild places. Boston: Beacon Press.

Namy, Laura L. & Gentner, D. (2002). Making a silk purse out of two sows' ears: Young children's use of comparison in category learning. Journal of Experimental Psychology: General, 131, 5–15.

Sewell, Laura (1999). Sight and sensibility: The ecopsychology of perception. New York, NY: Jeremy P. Tarcher/Putnam.

Thomashow, Mitchell (1995). Ecological identity: Becoming a reflective environmentalist. Cambridge, MA: MIT Press.

Young, Jon (1996). Seeing through native eyes: Understanding the language of nature. Duvall, WA: Wilderness Awareness School.

Young, Jon (1998). Kamana Naturalist Training, Level 1. Duvall, WA: Wilderness Awareness School.

Young, Jon & Haas, Ellen (1997). The art of mentoring and coyote tracking. Duvall, WA: Wilderness Awareness School Teweya Productions.

Chapter Seven: Generous Mentors' Spirits

Brown, Lyn Mikel and Gilligan, Carol (1992) Meeting at the Crossroads: Women's payshology and girls' development. New York: Ballantine Books.

Brown, Lyn Mikel (2004). As found on the internet: http://www.mainelygirls.org/reports/zones.html.

Coloroso, Barbara (1994). Kids are worth it: Giving your child the gift of inner discipline. New York: William Morrow.

Delis-Abrams, A. (1999). Attitudes, beliefs and choices: Simple, practical and playful messages about life. Coeur d'Alene, ID: ABC Feelings, Audio.

Gilligan, Carol, Janie V. Ward, J. M. Taylor, & B. Bardige (1988). (Eds.). Mapping the moral domain: A contribution of women's thinking to psychological theory and education. Cambridge, MA: Harvard University Graduate School of Education.

Hancock, Emily (1989). The girl within: Recapture the childhood self, the key to female identity. New York: E. P. Dutton.

Harter, Susan (2004). The cognitive and social construction of the developing self. New York: Guilford Press.

Hay, Louise L. (1992). The Power is Within You. Carlsbad, CA: Hay House

Huang, Chungliang Al & Jerry Lynch (1995). Mentoring: The Tao of giving and receiving wisdom. San Francisco: Harper San Francisco.

Pipher, Mary (1994). Reviving Ophelia: Saving the selves of adolescent girls. New York: Ballantine.

Pipher, Mary (1996). The shelter of each other: Rebuilding our families. New York: G.P. Putnam's Sons.

Sinetar, Marsha (1997). The mentor's spirit: Life lessons on leadership and the art of encouragement. Boulder, CO: Sounds True.

Young, Jon & Haas, Ellen (1997). The art of mentoring and coyote tracking. Duvall, WA: Wilderness Awareness School Teweya Productions.

Chapter Eight: Wrapping the Bundle: You as Woman

Estés, Clarissa Pinkola (1992). Women who run with the wolves.: Myths and stories of the Wild Woman archetype. New York: Ballantine Books.

Estés, Clarissa Pinkola (1995). Theater of the imagination, Volume 1. Boulder, CO: Sounds True.

Estés, Clarissa Pinkola (1995). Theater of the imagination, Volume 2. Boulder, CO: Sounds True.

LaChapelle, Dolores (1978). Earth Wisdom. Los Angeles: Guild of Tutors Press.

LaChapelle, Dolores (1992). Toward and understanding of psychology as the study of the relationship between nature within and nature without. Contemporary Philosophy, 12(8), 10–14.

LaChapelle, Dolores (1988). Sacred land, sacred sex, rapture of the deep: Concerning deep ecology and celebrating life. Silverton, CO: Finn Hill Arts.

LaChapelle, Dolores (2004) As found on the internet: http://www.context.org/ICLIB/IC05/LaChapel.htm

Nhât Hanh, Thich (1992). Peace Is Every Step : The Path of Mindfulness in Everyday Life. Gardena, CA: SCB Distributors

Myss, Carolyn (1996). Energy Anatomy: The science of personal power, spirituality, and health. Boulder, CO: Sounds True.

Starhawk (1989). The Spiral Dance: A Rebirth of the Ancient Religion of the Great Goddess. San Francisco, CA: Harper San Francisco.

Stone, Merlin (1990). Ancient Mirrors of Womanhood: A Treasury of Goddess and Heroine Lore from Around the World. Boston, MA: Beacon Press.

Woodman, Marion, Kate Danson, Mary Hamilton & Rita Greer Allen (1992). Leaving my father's house: A journey to conscious feminity. Boston, MA: Shambhala Publications.

Woodman, Marion (1993). Conscious feminity: Interviews with Marion Woodman. Toronto, Canada: Inner City Books.

Our website, www.womenmentoringgirls.org
offers the story board for each girl's
initiation ceremony to be reported
and so much more.

A robust one day workshop training
for women's archetypal role models
we playfully call *Her Feet on the Earth: Girls' Path to Womanhood*
intertwines circles and nature exploration for girls.
This national workshop led by women for women and girls
will be touring the country
and could be presented to your group near your home.
Consider the community of women around you,
check out the website,
then invite us to present our workshop to your community.

Delightfully optimistic about our future,

Gail Burkett, Ph.D.
PO Box 924
Donnelly, Idaho 83615
drwind@kennyoart.com

0-595-32454-1

Lightning Source UK Ltd.
Milton Keynes UK
UKOW03f2123060217

293747UK00001B/132/P